Democracies and Republics Between Past and Future

I0123547

Democracies and Republics Between Past and Future focuses on the concepts of direct rule by the people in early and classical Athens and the tribunician negative power in early republican Rome – and through this lens explores current political issues in our society.

This volume guides readers through the current constitutional systems in the Western world in an attempt to decipher the reasons and extent of the decline of the nexus between 'elections' and 'democracy'; it then turns its gaze to the past in search of some answers for the future, examining early and classical Athens and, finally, early republican Rome. In discussing Athens, it explores how an authentic 'power of the people' is more than voting and something rather different from representation, while the examples of Rome demonstrate – thanks to the paradigm of the so-called tribunician power – the importance of institutionalised mechanisms of dialogic conflict between competing powers.

This book will be of primary interest to scholars of legal history, both recent and ancient, and to classicists, but also to the more general reader with an interest in politics and history.

Carlo Pelloso is Associate Professor of Roman Law at the University of Verona, Italy, and Adjunct Professor of Ancient Greek Law at the University of Padua, Italy. He has been 'visiting scholar' at the Universities of Edinburgh, UK; Berlin (Freie Universität; Humboldt Universität), Germany; and La Habana, Cuba. He has published more than fifty articles and four monographs on the legal experiences of the ancient Mediterranean. He is co-director of the international review *RΔE – Review of Hellenic Law*.

Routledge Focus on Classical Studies

This new series, part of the Routledge Focus short-form programme, provides a venue for the most up-to-date research in the field of Classical Studies. The series covers a range of topics, from focussed studies on specific texts, figures, or themes, to works on wider issues.

Prophets, Prophecy, and Oracles in the Roman Empire
Jewish, Christian, and Greco-Roman Cultures
Leslie Kelly

Theophrastus' *Characters*
A New Introduction
Sonia Pertsinidis

Gallus Reborn
A Study of the Diffusion and Reception of Works Ascribed to Gaius Cornelius Gallus
Paul White

Democracies and Republics Between Past and Future
From the Athenian Agora to e-Democracy, from the Roman Republic to Negative Power
Carlo Pelloso

For more information about this series, please visit: https://www.routledge.com/Routledge-Focus-on-Classical-Studies/book-series/FOCUSCLSS

Democracies and Republics Between Past and Future

From the Athenian Agora to
e-Democracy, from the Roman
Republic to Negative Power

Carlo Pelloso

Routledge
Taylor & Francis Group

LONDON AND NEW YORK

First published 2021
by Routledge
2 Park Square, Milton Park, Abingdon, Oxon OX14 4RN

and by Routledge
605 Third Avenue, New York, NY 10017

Routledge is an imprint of the Taylor & Francis Group, an informa business

British Library Cataloguing-in-Publication Data
A catalogue record for this book is available from the British Library

Library of Congress Cataloging-in-Publication Data
Names: Pelloso, Carlo, author. Title: Democracies and republics between past and future : from the Athenian agora to e-democracy, from the Roman Republic to negative power / Carlo Pelloso. Description: Abingdon, Oxon ; New York, NY : Routledge, 2021. | Series: Routledge focus on classical studies | Includes bibliographical references and index. | Identifiers: LCCN 2020043954 (print) | LCCN 2020043955 (ebook) | ISBN 9780367672591 (hardback) | ISBN 9780367672607 (paperback) | ISBN 9781003130505 (ebook) Subjects: LCSH: Democracy--History. | Republics. | Athens (Greece) --Politics and government. | Rome--Politics and government--510-30 B.C. Classification: LCC JC421 .P39 2021 (print) | LCC JC421 (ebook) | DDC 321.8--dc23
LC record available at https://lccn.loc.gov/2020043954
LC ebook record available at https://lccn.loc.gov/2020043955

ISBN 13: 978-0-367-67259-1 (hbk)
ISBN 13: 978-0-367-67260-7 (pbk)

Typeset in Sabon
by SPi Global, India

To Mario:

Do not forget that "everything not saved will be lost" (as the Nintendo Quit Screen Message says).

Contents

Introduction
Democracies, republics and beyond: Challenges and questions

Democracy, both on paper and in real life, is currently under attack from many fronts. Democracy remains an unchallenged set of ideals as both a counter-power which seeks to curb the hegemony of those with elite status and a system designed to respond to the preferences of the wider general populace; yet there can be no doubt that the current legal systems which claim to operate as genuine democracies have been, and continue to be, vigorously criticised, almost universally.[1] Political scientists, historians, and lawyers – who have abandoned the 'golden models' shaped by advocates of a barely normativistic reading of our constitutional apparatuses[2] – show increasing awareness that democracy can also take on illiberal traits,[3] thereby often adopting a realistic, if not pessimistic, approach to interpreting the empirical findings of their research on the crisis of legitimacy affecting liberal representative systems.

Far from idealising the instruments and objectives of 'democracy' *qua talis*, the new realism trend has highlighted two fundamental 'challenges' – not to say 'threats' – considered inherent in the democratic apparatus of today: these are the interconnected challenges of the 'oligarchic' and the 'epistemic' systems.[4]

Under an oligarchy, the current democratic process would not reflect the preferences of the median voter. Conversely, such process would lead to an oligarchic bias, its outcomes being aligned with the interests of the socio-economic elites able to bypass popular scrutiny and thereby enact public policy through non-electoral mechanisms[5]: a shadowy minority would re-emerge, prompting evocative mottos, such as Occupy Wall Street's "We are the 99%," and exacerbating the populistic dualism of the ordinary versus the establishment, as evidenced by the great success of movements such as Podemos and the M5S (Five Star Movement).[6]

However, within an epistemic regime, voters could neither select policies nor leaders. Rather, their vote would be based – primarily, if not entirely – on their 'group identity': in other words, citizens would tend not to make well-informed and deliberate decisions on policy issues and would normally be unable to deploy the ballot box as a means to secure effectual accountability over the constitutional power.[7] Awareness of the futility of voting, alongside the consolidation of neoliberal individualism,[8] would not only maximise electoral absenteeism, apathy and intolerance of procedures but also enhance both the withdrawal of political decisions to the private sector and the withdrawal of individuals to tend to their immediate and private needs: that is to say, people – neglecting Aristotle – would cease to be political animals.

Within this framework permeated by 'biased pluralism'[9] and irrational and myopic voting,[10] responses to these two challenges have taken different forms within different groups. At times, the aim has been to push the line further and, accordingly, to reinforce democracy via 'plebeian' and 'antagonistic' solutions, pivoting on plebiscites and referenda.[11] At other times, attempts have been made to condemn and go beyond the current democratic model as purportedly concealing an ineffective and dangerous 'mob-cracy.'[12] Yet between these two antithetical poles, three main routes have been followed.

On the one hand, if the solutions directly or indirectly hostile to democracy *per se* are abandoned, then someone has claimed to "identify procedurally democratic nudges or barriers to counteract such forces of clannishness and emotion,"[13] and someone else has claimed to "provide more and better education" as the best strategy "for more democracy and civic participation."[14]

On the other hand, some 'epistocratic' and 'elitist' correctives (for instance, weighted voting) have been proposed, endorsing projects inclined to favour the so-called top decile, yet without buttressing a genuine return to the minority rule.[15]

Finally, as elections have often proven to miss the ideal of 'anti-oligarchic responsiveness' and to amount to 'judgments on the past' rather than to 'choices of orientation,' one has claimed that, by strengthening the three main powers of the so-called counter-democracy (i.e. oversight, prevention, and judgment), critical sovereignty could both integrate "a system capable of giving adequate expression to democratic experience" and institutionalise an authentic 'democratic distrust' (not to be confused with banal and unpolitical forms of opposition and populism).[16]

Democracy is thought of as a set of institutions which have always been in crisis and, at the same time, a generally uncontested set of universal ideals.[17] Political theory, from its initial stages to contemporary studies, stresses that democracy itself is not conceivable without a crisis.[18] Currently, under the veil of elections, the 'government of the people' is akin to an elderly woman on her deathbed. While the people try to make themselves heard through their shouts and their silences, the whispering of the oligarchic power seeps in. So, the dilemma is: should we keep the elderly woman alive or let her die? Do we curb the shouting or eradicate the background noise? Do we try to involve those who are silent or consider this an act of selflessness?

Indeed, the current 'ontological' crisis could become a pre-condition which prompts the possible return of some of those traits which were once considered essential within an authentically participatory and deliberative democracy[19] – namely, the direct, free, and equal involvement of the δῆμος in its collective decision-making capacity. As such, decisions made directly by voters could better reflect their views and, accordingly, solve the 'principal-agent problem'; additionally, the ability to vote on a given issue without representatives, but with the support of sufficient information and after adequate deliberation, would enhance the opportunity to serve the best interest of the community. Furthermore, a genuine democracy would enhance public self-expression and thereby constitute the means to fulfil individual and collective freedom. The 5th- and 4th-century πόλις of Athens is an excellent example of this, embodying a government designed to achieve not only the highest level of popular participation but also demonstrates the enactment of a deliberative stance through informed debates among citizens.[20]

Yet the oligarchic challenge remains a significant obstacle which direct forms of democracy can seek to navigate but cannot fully overcome. The epistemic shortcomings that at present affect the public[21] and, thereby, permit manipulation[22] remain untouched by the implementation of participatory institutions that empower citizens without offering resources to counteract the threats associated with the elite monopoly (which, for instance, can continue to threaten democratic equality by influencing public policy through the ownership of mass media or even by means of philanthropic activity, serving as officeholders, lobbying candidates and administrators through interest-group activity). Indeed, "the crisis of political accountability that besets contemporary democracy demands institutional means through which economic and political elites are actively contested instead of those that conceal and sustain the entrenchment of their privilege and prerogative."[23]

Thus on the one side, ancient Athens presents a prominent case study for direct democracy on a mass scale. On the other, it is the construction of the Roman *res publica* as *res populi*, alongside the extraordinary role played – mainly at the outset – by the *tribuni plebis* through their 'negative power,'[24] which provides an extensive source of insight into the approaches taken to minimise or constrain the oligarchic influence on the public realm and, accordingly, to foster democratic modes of political equality and liberty that appear to be as removed from the theory and practice of the 'separation of powers' as possible.[25]

Against this background, this book will look to the past not so much to understand the present crisis but to find inspiration for the future.

The first chapter will focus on the so-called English or Gothic model – i.e. a form of constitutionalism that still represents (although no longer adequate, in many ways, to deal with the demands of the contemporary Western world) a crucial point of reference. This model – involving both the 'representation' policy as a form of sovereignty wielded via the assembly's vote and the 'separation' principle as a constitutional device directed to contrast governmental abuses – will be evaluated in its fundamental traits and with regard to its main conceptual and historical flaws.

From this starting point, I will look to the classical world not only to highlight its diversity of context and practice from today but also to demonstrate how we can make the most of the richness of ideas embedded in the past for today and tomorrow.

In the second chapter, I will sketch – from a procedural and theoretical perspective – the dynamics of Athenian decision making, stressing how relevant equality, cohesion and solidarity – i.e. the main values underpinning the democratic institutions – were within the δῆμος, as well as how indispensable the assiduous, committed and broad-based popular participation was for the working of the political machinery.

In the third chapter, I will reflect on the so-called Roman model of government: pivoting on the concrete notion of *populus* as an indivisible sovereign that cannot be represented (but only served) and implying the *tribuni plebis'* negative power as an extra-constitutional expedient directed to curb the establishment and to reduce inequality. As such, it represents a further answer – a 'republican answer' – to the crisis of legitimacy of our current liberal and representative democracies.

For the moment, however, I will settle with leaving my readers with a challenging question:

> Imagine having to develop a system today that would express the will of the people. Would it really be a good idea to have them all queue up at polling stations every four or five years with a bit of card in their hands and go into a dark booth to put a mark next to names on a list, names of people about whom restless reporting had been going on for months in a commercial environment that profits from restlessness?[26]

Notes

1 It is remarkable that the *Democracy Index* published by the *Intelligence Unit of The Economist* (2018) shows that support for democracy and free speech is rapidly fading: among the 167 countries listed, only 19 could be considered full democracies. Cf. Salvadori 2011.

2 According to the 'folk theory,' well-informed citizens are capable of both translating their choices into public policies by selecting leaders responsible to their will and enforcing retrospective accountability (see Schumpeter 1942; Key 1966; Dahl 1989).

3 As is well-known, Zakaria 1997, argued that as of the mid-1970s, democracy in the form of free elections spread to countries which previously lacked a liberal tradition of a commitment to constitutionalism, the rule of law and individual rights: The result was the rise of regimes which, although formally democratic, could not be considered authentic liberal democracies. Prime Minister Viktor Orbán's Speech at the 25th Bálványos Summer Free University and Student Camp, November 26, 2014, is practically the manifesto of an illiberal democracy *in fieri*: cf. Uitz 2015: 284. After the Hungarian 'unconstitutional constitution' (Scheppele 2012) was approved, the European Parliament asked European Union (EU) member states to determine, in accordance with Treaty Article 7, whether Hungary was at risk of breaching the EU's founding values. This was the first time that the European Parliament called on the Council to act against a member state in order to prevent a potentially serious threat to the Union itself: cf. the European Parliament resolution of 12 September 2018 (2017/2131[INL].)

4 Such a dual critique – based on empirical data, although conducted within a framework which sought to defend democratic ideals – seems to be so intense that one could even question whether 'realism' of this type is compatible with 'democracy': "I struggle to see how one can be a realist...and still maintain a commitment to anything resembling democracy" (Ahlstrom-Vij 2018: 11).

5 Bartels 2018 demonstrates that contemporary democracies tend to track the interests of the more affluent populace and thus to be more responsive to their preferences. Moreover, provided that there was a significant degree of cohesion among the socio-economic elite populace, ordinary citizens would be under-represented and, therefore, would have a "statistically non-significant impact upon public policy": this would lead to "nearly total failure of 'median voter'" (Gilens - Page 2014: 575; cf. also Gilens 2012).

6 Urbinati 2019: 158 ff.; cf. Eatwell - Goodwin 2018: 117 ff.; 123 f.; see Urbinati 2014 on the difference existing between popular movements (which have no project of populist power) and populisms (viewed both as movements and new disfigured forms of representative government).

7 Achen - Bartels 2016: 7; 12; 311; 319 believe that "conventional democratic ideals amount to fairy tales,' which 'collapsed in the face of modern, social scientific research." The outcomes of their study show that "voters choose a party validating their social and political identities" and their commitment to specific policies would be as limited, given that it mirrors group identity. As such, a democratic election would have "little real policy content." For recent epistemic defences of democracy, see Landemore 2013; Poblet - Casanovas - Rodríguez-Doncel 2019.

8 See, among others, Judt 2010.

9 Gilens - Page 2014: 567 f.

10 Lodge - Taber 2013.

11 Mouffe 2000: 80 ff.; Laclau - Mouffe 2001: 149 ff.; Mouffe: 2005; Laclau 2005a; Laclau 2005b: 22 ff.; Frank 2010; McCormick 2011; Breaugh 2013; Hamilton 2014; Green 2016; Arlen 2019; Mulvad - Stahl 2019; Vergara 2019. On the one hand, such instruments – one has stressed – formally resort to the direct "will of the people," which while allowing forms of direct democracy turn out to be substantially removed from the ideals of a deliberative democracy (cf. Offe 2017). On the other hand, it has been noted that all mass dictatorships start as 'populist movements,' which – demonstrating an array of democratic rights which undermine democratic principles and values – promote 'the people's voice' through referenda and plebiscites. At the same time, this supports the idea of direct representation between the people (or better the 'right' *pars* of the people) and the leader, viewed as an incarnation of all claims of the *pars* in power (see Urbinati 2019; cf. Müller 2011; Molyneux - Osborne 2017; Mounk 2018).

12 For instance, someone claimed that it is time for the elites to rise up against the ignorant masses: Traub 2016.

13 Cohen 2017: 153.

14 See Széll 2018: 213 (with further bibliography); cf. Landemore 2013; Landemore 2017; Landemore 2018.

15 In *Against Democracy*, Brennan, while acknowledging that "ideal epistocracy isn't a live option" (Brennan 2016: 207), promotes a version of epistocracy based on the so-called government by stimulated oracle – that is, a fresh interpretation of the aristocratic ideal of 'rule by guardians' (Brennan 2016: 220; cf. Arlen 2019).

16 Rosanvallon 2008: 173; 163. According to this scholar, counter-democracy is not "the opposite of democracy but rather a form of democracy

that reinforces the usual electoral democracy as a kind of buttress, a democracy of indirect powers disseminated throughout society – in other words, a durable democracy of distrust, which complements the episodic democracy of the usual electoral-representative system" (Rosanvallon 2008: 8). Moreover, such powers "exist only in relation to the central power, which they challenge in some ways and reinforce in others" (Rosanvallon 2008: 263).

17 Sen 1999.
18 Cf., for instance, Laski 1933; Held 1996: 13 ff.; Canfora 2006: 21 ff.; Keane 2009; De Simone 2015.
19 Deliberative democracy theorists tend to reject the compatibility of authentic deliberation and participatory democracies, despite often referring to the example of Athens: cf. Pateman 2012 and Sintomer 2011. Yet some recent studies seem not to rule out the possibility of coexistence of participatory and deliberative traits within the same democratic government: see Curato - Dryzek - Ercan - Hendriks - Niemeye 2017: 32. As far as Athens is concerned, Ober, emphasising the role played by deliberation in enhancing and unifying dispersed knowledge, argues that "democratic Athens depended directly and self-consciously on actively deploying the epistemic resources of its citizenry" (Ober 2012: 118); this author further notes that our current political practice "often treats free citizens as passive subjects by discounting the value of what they know" (Ober 2008: 1).
20 On participation, see Hansen 1991; Cartledge 2016: 105 ff.; Gagarin 2020: 10 ff. On deliberation, see Balot 2004: 63 ff.; Ober 2008: 160 ff.; Villacèque 2013; Koch 2014: 13; Canevaro 2018; Canevaro 2020; *contra*, see Hansen 1991: 142 ff.; Cammack 2013; Cammack 2017 (expected but unpublished); Cammack 2020.
21 On 'agnotology' (as the induction of doubts and ignorance), see Proctor - Schiebinger 2008. Cf. the *Freedom on the Net 2017 Report*, of Freedom House, https://freedomhouse.org/report/freedom-net/freedom-net-2017, with Shahbaz 2018. Suffice it to say that in recent years, according to the European Commission, online manipulation and misinformation tactics have been detected in an electoral context by at least 18 countries and misinformation tactics have contributed to a general decline in Internet freedom for the seventh consecutive year: COM (2018), 236 FINAL, 12. Moreover, according to the Oxford Internet Institute, in 2016, misinformation content from about 50,000 automatic Twitter accounts belonging to the International Research Agency (IRA) based in St. Petersburg reached about 126 million US citizens in the run-up to the presidential election: cf. Bellotti 2018.
22 For instance, taking into consideration the classical model, Fishkin 1993: 21 and 50 argues that small-scale democracies are "more vulnerable to tyranny" since they are "more vulnerable to demagoguery" and that increasing participation does not affect the quality of the participation, remaining "the deliberative competence of mass publics...suspect." Likewise, reflecting on the digital model, Gerbaudo 2019: 133 stresses the following: "Despite the presence of deliberative, discussion-oriented and qualitative forms of online decision-making, the form of digital democracy that prevails in digital parties is clearly top-down: more concerned with balloting than discussing and favouring representative and

plebiscitary democracy tendencies over deliberative democracy." In the so-called plebiscitarianism 2.0, a small leadership holds the power, and the role carved out for the base is to ratify by acclamation what has been decided by the leadership. Furthermore, it does not hesitate to use internal propaganda and to manipulate the issues at hand in order to achieve the desired results. On the difference between plebiscitarianism and populism, see Urbinati 2014: 182 ff.

23 McCormick 2017: 4.
24 See Catalano 1967a; Catalano 1967b; Catalano 1971: 32 f.; 59 ff.; 128 ff.; Catalano 2005; Catalano 2007; Catalano 2011. The scholar has recently devoted some dense pages to describing the ideological battle that he has pursued since the 1960s to the present day to overturn deep-rooted constitutionalism, which is traditionally based on the separation of powers and the renewal of the system involving negative power: see Catalano 2018.
25 McCormick 2011, in an innovative study inspired by Machiavelli's analysis of the Roman republic, has emphasised the latter's anti-aristocratic and radically democratic thinking and, in modelling a Machiavellian democracy, has suggested resorting to a "People's Tribunate." It would consist of an assembly composed of non-wealthy citizens selected by lottery for a one-year term, vested with several oversight powers (such as to veto one national legislative proposal or to initiate impeachment proceedings against the lawmaker). In addition, following the way paved by McCormick, Hamilton 2014 has both rejected the view that conflates Machiavelli's ideas with an account of freedom conceived of as non-interference, or absence of constraint, and has maintained that Machiavelli supported the connection between popular power and the creation of "separate and class-specific institutions for wealthy and non-wealthy citizens." Machiavelli was indeed a pivotal source of inspiration for the theories developed by Babeuf and, especially, by Rousseau on the grounds of the so-called Roman model of constitutionalism (see Catalano 1971: 37 ff.; 59 ff.): in search of new horizons for constitutionalism, his pamphlet *The Social Contract* has often been used as a theoretical, if not practical, paradigm as opposed to the English model and, at the same time, informed by the constitutional engineering of the Romans (on these two types of constitutionalism, see Catalano 2013; cf. Catalano 1996: 20; Catalano 2011: 31; see, moreover, Lobrano 1996: 194 ff.; Dubouchet 2001; Lobrano 2004; Lobrano 2018).
26 Van Reybrouck 2016.

Bibliography

C.H. Achen, L. Bartels, *Democracy for Realists*, New Jersey, 2016.
K. Ahlstrom-Vij, Is Democracy an Option for the Realist?, *Critical Review: A Journal of Politics and Society* 30 (2018), 1–12.
G. Arlen, Aristotle and the Problem of Oligarchic Harm: Insights for Democracy, *European Journal of Political Theory* 18 (2019), 393–414.

S. Bagg, The Power of the Multitude: Answering Epistemic Challenges to Democracy, *American Political Science Review* 112 (2018), 891–904.

R. Balot, *Greek Political Thought*, Oxford, 2004.

R. Bellotti, Propaganda e manipolazione nelle elezioni politiche: il ruolo dei social network e degli algoritmi basati sulla intelligenza artificiale, *Menabò* 88 (July 17, 2018): https://www.eticaeconomia.it/propaganda-e-manipolazione-nelle-elezioni-politiche-il-ruolo-dei-social-network-e-degli-algoritmi-basati-sulla-intelligenza-artificiale/.

L. Bartels, *Unequal Democracy: The Political Economy of the New Gilded Age*[2], Princeton/Oxford, 2018.

M. Breaugh, *The Plebeian Experience: A Discontinuous History of Political Freedom*, New York, 2013.

J. Brennan, *Against Democracy*, Princeton/Oxford, 2016.

D. Cammack, Aristotle on the Virtue of the Multitude, *Political Theory* 41 (2013), 175–202.

D. Cammack, The Democratic Significance of the Classical Athenian Courts, in *Decline: Decadence, Decay and Decline in History and Society*, ed. W. O'Reilly, Budapest, 2017 (expected but unpublished).

D. Cammack, Deliberation in Ancient Greek Assemblies, *Classical Philology* 115 (2020), 486–522.

M. Canevaro, Majority Rule vs. *consensus*: The Practice of Democratic Deliberation in the Greek *poleis*, in *Ancient Greek History and the Contemporary Social Sciences*, eds. M. Canevaro, A. Erskine, B. Gray and J. Ober, Edinburgh, 2018, 101–156.

M. Canevaro, La délibération démocratique à l'Assemblée athénienne: Procédures et stratégies de légitimation, *Annales. Histoire, Sciences Sociales* 74.2 (2020), 339–381.

L. Canfora, *Democracy in Europe: A History of an Ideology (making of Europe)*, Oxford, 2006.

B. Caplan, *The Myth of the Rational Voter: Why Democracies Choose Bad Policies*, New Jersey, 2007.

P. Cartledge, *Democracy: A Life*, Oxford, 2016.

P. Catalano, *"Potere negativo" e sovranità dei cittadini nell'età tecnologica*, in *Engagement et responsabilité des anciens élèves dans un monde en transformation, II Congressus Unionis Mundialis Antiquorum Societatis Jesu Alumnorum, Romae 26–30 Augusti*, Actes, Napoli, 1967a, 91–106.

P. Catalano, *"Potere negativo" e sovranità popolare*, in *I cattolici italiani nei tempi nuovi della cristianità, Atti del convegno di studio della Democrazia Cristiana, Lucca 28–30 aprile 1967*, ed. G. Rossini, Roma, 1967b, 824–830.

P. Catalano, *Tribunato e resistenza*, Torino, 1971.

P. Catalano, Divisione del potere e potere popolare, *Ius Antiquum* 1 (1996), 19–27.

P. Catalano, Sovranità della *multitudo* e potere negativo: un aggiornamento, in *Studi in onore di G. Ferrara*, I, Torino, 2005, 658–661.

P. Catalano, Postilla al «Promemoria», *Diritto@Storia* 6 (2007): http://www. dirittoestoria.it/6/Memorie/Tribunato_della_Plebe/Catalano-Postilla-al-Promemoria-storico-giuridico.htm.

P. Catalano, Constitutionnalisme latin et constitution de la République romaine de 1848 (à propos du droit public romain du tribunat), in *Constitutions, républiques, mémoires. 1849 entre Rome et la France*, ed. L. Reverso, Paris, 2011, 29–57.

P. Catalano, Rousseau et le droit public romain, in *Rousseau, le droit et l'histoire des institutions, Actes du Colloque international pour le Tricentenaire de la naissance de Jean-Jacques Rousseau 1712–1778, organisé à Genève, 12–14 septembre 2012*, eds. A. Dufour, F. Quastana and V. Monnier, Genève/Zurich/Bâle, 2013, 3–27.

P. Catalano, L'appoggio di Giuseppe Grosso: dalle lezioni del 1953 alle ricerche sull'America Latina, in *Tribunado – Poder negativo y defensa de los derechos humanos. Segundas Jornadas Ítalo-Latinoamericanas de Defensores Cívicos y Defensores del Puebl. En homenaje al Profesor Giuseppe Grosso (Torino, 8–9 settembre 2016)*, ed. A. Trisciuoglio, Milano, 2018, 24–29.

E.F. Cohen, A Discussion of Achen and Bartels' Democracy for Realists: Why Elections Do Not Produce Responsive Government, *Perspectives on Politics* 15 (2017), 152–153.

N. Curato, J.S. Dryzek, S.A. Ercan, C.M. Hendriks, S. Niemeye, Twelve Key Findings in Deliberative Democracy Research, *Daedalus* 146.3 (2017), 28–38.

R.A. Dahl, *Democracy and Its Critics*, New Haven/London, 1989.

R. Eatwell, M. Goodwin, *National Populism. The Revolt Against Liberal Democracy*, London, 2018.

R. De Simone, *Come la democrazia fallisce*, Milano, 2015.

P. Dubouchet, *De Montesquieu le Moderne à Rousseau l'Ancien. La démocratie et la république en question*, Paris/Montreal/Budapest/Torino, 2001.

J. Fishkin, *Democracy and Deliberation: New Directions for Democratic Reform*, New Haven, 1993.

M. Gagarin, *Democratic Law in Classical Athens*, Austin, 2020.

P. Gerbaudo, *The Digital Party. Political Organisation and Online Democracy*, London, 2019.

M. Gilens, *Affluence and Influence*, New York/New Jersey, 2012.

M. Gilens, B.I. Page, Testing Theories of American Politics: Elites, Interest Groups, and Average Citizens, *Perspectives on Politics* 12 (2014), 564–581.

J. Green, *The Shadow of Unfairness: A Plebeian Theory of Liberal Democracy*, New York, 2016.

L. Hamilton, *Freedom is Power: Liberty Through Political Representation*, Cambridge, 2014.

M.H. Hansen, *The Athenian Democracy in the Age of Demosthenes*, Oxford, 1991.

D. Held, *Models of Democracy*, Oxford, 1996.

J. Frank, *Constituent Moments: Enacting the People in Postrevolutionary America*, Durham, 2010.

T. Judt, *Ill Fares the Land: A Treatise on Our Present Discontents*, London, 2010.

J. Keane, *Life and Death of Democracy*, New York, 2009.

V.O. Jr. Key, *The Responsible Electorate: Rationality in Presidential Voting, 1936–1960*, Harvard, 1966.

N. Kolodny, How People Vote, *Boston Review* (February 17, 2017): http://bostonreview.net/politics/niko-kolodny-how-people-vote.

C. Koch, Aristotle on deliberation, in *Let's Talk Politics: New Essays on Deliberative Rhetoric*, eds. H. Van Belle, K. Rutten, P. Gillaerts, D. Van De Mieroop and B. Van Gorp, Amsterdam/Philadelphia, 2014, 13–25.

E. Laclau, C. Mouffe, Hegemony and Radical Democracy, in *Hegemony and Socialist Strategy: Toward a Radical Democratic Politics*[2], eds. E. Laclau and C. Mouffe, London, 2001, 149–194.

E. Laclau, Populism: What's in a Name, in *Populism and the Mirror of Democracy*, ed. F. Panizza, London, 2005a, 22–49.

E. Laclau, *On Populist Reason*, London, 2005b.

H. Landemore, *Democratic Reason. Politics, Collective Intelligence, and the Rule of the Many*, Princeton, 2013.

H. Landemore, Beyond the Fact of Disagreement? The Epistemic Turn in Deliberative Democracy, *Social Epistemology* 31.3 (2017), 277–295.

H. Landemore, Referendums Are Never Merely Referendums: On the Need to Make Popular Vote Processes More Deliberative, *Swiss Political Science Review* 24.3 (2018), 320–327.

H.J. Laski, *Democracy in Crisis*, London, 1933.

G. Lobrano, 'Res publica res populi'. *La legge e la limitazione del potere*, Torino, 1996.

G. Lobrano, La *respublica* romana, municipale-federativa e tribunizia: modello costituzionale attuale, *Diritto@Storia* 3 (2004): http://www.dirittoestoria.it/3/Memorie/Organizzare-ordinamento/Lobrano-Res-publica-Romana-modello-costituzionale-attuale.htm.

G. Lobrano, "Mezzi per la difesa della libertà" e "forme di governo", in *Tribunado – Poder negativo y defensa de los derechos humanos. Segundas Jornadas Ítalo-Latinoamericanas de Defensores Cívicos y Defensores del Puebl. En homenaje al Profesor Giuseppe Grosso (Torino, 8–9 settembre 2016)*, ed. A. Trisciuoglio, Milano, 2018, 185–236.

M. Lodge, C.S. Taber, *The Rationalizing Voter*, Cambridge, 2013.

J. McCormick, *Machiavellian Democracy*, Cambridge, 2011.

J. McCormick, Rousseau's Rome and the Repudiation of Populist Republicanism, *Critical Review of International Social and Political Philosophy* 10 (2017), 3–27.

M. Molyneux, T. Osborne, Populism: A Deflationary View, *Economy and Society* 46.1 (2017), 1–19.

C. Mouffe, *Democratic Paradox*, London, 2000.

C. Mouffe, The 'End of Politics' and the Challenge of Right-Wing Populism, in *Populism and the Mirror of Democracy*, ed. F. Panizza, London, 2005, 50–71.

Y. Mounk, *The People vs. Democracy. Why Our Freedom Is in Danger and How to Save It*, Cambridge, 2018.

J.-W. Müller, *Contesting Democracy. Political Ideas in Twentieth-Century Europe*, New Haven, 2011.

A.M. Mulvad, R.H. Stahl, Civilizing Left Populism: Towards a Theory of Plebeian Democracy, *Constellations* 26 (2019), 591–606.

J. Ober, *Democracy and Knowledge: Innovation and Learning in Classical Athens*, Princeton, 2008.

J. Ober, Epistemic Democracy in Classical Athens, in *Collective Wisdom: Principles and Mechanisms*, eds. H. Landemore and J. Elster, Cambridge, 2012, 118–146.

C. Offe, Referendum vs. Institutionalized Deliberation: What Democratic Theorists Can Learn from the 2016 Brexit Decision, *Daedalus* 146.3 (2017), 14–27.

C. Pateman, Participatory Democracy Revisited, *Perspectives On Politics* 10.1 (2012), 7–19.

M. Poblet, P. Casanovas, V. Rodríguez-Doncel, *Linked Democracy. Foundations, Tools, and Applications*, New York, 2019.

R.N. Proctor, L. Schiebinger (eds.), *Agnotology. The Making and Unmaking of Ignorance*, Stanford, 2008.

P. Rosanvallon, *Counter-Democracy: Politics in an Age of Distrust*, trans., Cambridge, 2008.

M.L. Salvadori, *Democrazie senza democrazia*, Roma/Bari, 2011.

K.L. Scheppele, The Unconstitutional Constitution, *Krugman Blogs -The New York Times* (January 2, 2012): https://krugman.blogs.nytimes.com/2012/01/02/the-unconstitutional-constitution/.

J. Schumpeter, *Capitalism, Socialism, and Democracy*, New York, 1942.

A. Sen, Democracy as a Universal Value, *Journal of Democracy* 10.3 (1999), 3–17.

A. Shahbaz, Fake News, Data Collection, and the Challenge to Democracy, *Freedom House, Freedom on the Net 2018. The Rise of Digital Authoritarianism* (October 31, 2018): https://freedomhouse.org/report/freedom-net/freedom-net-2018/rise-digital-authoritarianism.

Y. Sintomer, Délibération et participation: affinité élective ou concepts en tension?, *Participations* 1 (2011), 239–276.

G. Széll, Democracy and Participation in the Twenty-First Century, *International Review of Sociology* 28.2 (2018), 209–215.

J. Traub, It's Time for the Elites to Rise up Against the Ignorant Masses, *Foreign Policy* (June 28, 2016): https://foreignpolicy.com/2016/06/28/its-time-for-the-elites-to-rise-up-against-ignorant-masses-trump-2016-brexit/.

R. Uitz, Can You Tell When an Illiberal Democracy is in the Making? An Appeal to Comparative Constitutional Scholarship from Hungary, *I-CON* 13.1 (2015), 279–300.

N. Urbinati, *Democracy Disfigured: Opinion, Truth, and the People*, Cambridge/London, 2014.

N. Urbinati, *Me the People: How Populism Transforms Democracy*, Cambridge/London, 2019.

R. Van Reybrouck, Why Elections Are Bad for Democracy, *The Guardian* (June 29, 2016): www.theguardian.com/politics/2016/jun/29why-elections-are-bad-for-democracy.

C. Vergara, Populism as Plebeian Politics: Inequality, Domination, and Popular Empowerment, *Journal of Political Philosophy* 28 (2019), 222–246.

N. Villacèque, *Spectateurs de paroles: délibération démocratique et théâtre à Athènes à l'époque Classique*, Rennes, 2013.

F. Zakaria, The Rise of Illiberal Democracy, *Foreign Affairs* 76.6 (1997), 22–43.

1 The need for new paradigms

1.1 The crumbling constitution

It is not surprising that a variety of the symptoms of the crisis affecting our contemporary political reality are found in dystopian and apocalyptic narratives. The sick liquidity of today's world bodes well for 'antidotes' that are as solid as they are disturbing: these narratives do not predict the transformation of the world to a new and other reality but the altered and exaggerated state of current affairs.[1]

Many authors have created futuristic settings by drawing inspiration from current events to inform their themes, plot development and characterisation, particularly since the end of the Cold War and the rise of capitalist democracy. The reality of our hi-tech world, devoted to our private lives, as opposed to the public sphere, and enmeshed in a totalising market, has become a prolific source of inspiration for movies and novels. Under the surface of more or less baroque scenarios, which are transfigured together with our anxieties, fears and expectations, two opposing pictures clearly emerge: a shining world of greedy corporations and a charred world of post-technological hunters.

On the one hand, dystopian works present the disturbing reality of the current Western order under a perfected authoritarian or totalitarian rule; on the other hand, apocalyptic literature explores the deterioration of our known reality beyond recognition after the breakdown of the current order and triumph of anarchy. These two hypothetical worlds erode all of the distinguishing traits of our 'critical' era and project civilisations, which are founded on the extreme amplification of the liberalisation of trade and commodification of natural resources, on the expansion of human roles, on enhancements in digital technology and genetic science and on the return of governmental authorities to their police powers, along with mistrust in politics and individualism. The fear that new economic Leviathans shall devour the post-Westphalian sovereignties with increasing ferocity is melded with the exploitation of Margaret Thatcher's neoliberal *dictum* "there is no such thing as society. There is [a] living tapestry of men and women…and the quality of our lives will depend upon how much each of us is prepared to take responsibility for ourselves."[2]

All in all, the literary portrayals of our society depict the democratic ideals of freedom and equality as unattainable; there is no autonomous body of 'the people' and 'the power,' whether institutionalised or *de facto*, is totally unrestrained. Is it possible to prevent utopia and dystopia from overwhelming our lives? What efforts can we make to improve 'democracy' through radical, yet feasible, institutional reforms? Is a frontal assault on both over-domination and apathy conceivable? Can we lay the foundations for a future world where the inert mass shall be replaced by an active people?

1.2 Post-democracy

Conferences entitled "Representation and Renewal" or "Is the Party Over?"[3] well attest to the growing political and legal interest in retrospectively analysing and better comprehending the current crisis with a view to overcoming it;[4] however, some authors have already projected their sight beyond the corpse of democracy towards a 'post-democratic' future, among them, Colin Crouch.[5] According to Crouch, the democratic golden age of the liberal and representative democracies of Western Europe and North America have long since passed. Globalisation, deregulation and the loss of collective organisational capacity within society have all affected democracy. It is true that formal processes and institutions of democracy continue to exist, but they are rapidly becoming a box that has lost its contents: important questions of economic and financial politics are no longer decided by democratically elected political bodies but by global companies, banks and deregulated markets; money and lobbying penetrate parties and election campaigns; medialisation and manipulation of politics have become common realities.

While Crouch sees the cause of the problems facing democratic legitimacy in the triumph of neoliberal capitalism, Wolfgang Merkel denies that the qualities of democracy have declined over the last decade and that instead we can speak of a wholesale crisis of democracy. Merkel has identified three categories of challenges which face our current democracies: (1) capitalism as a financial challenge to democratic nations, (2) supranationalism (globalisation, the European Union [EU]) as a challenge to the national democratic state and (3) socio-economic inequality as a challenge to the democratic principle of political equality.[6]

On the one hand, the citadel of the democratic ideals continues to resist, albeit under siege;[7] on the other, the constitutional systems that claim to endorse democracy – and almost everybody does: Vladimir Putin has declared Russia a "sovereign democracy" and even North Korea calls itself a "Democratic People's Republic" – have fragile walls, which, while yet to be torn down, are nevertheless unstable: yet "You can fool all the people some of the time, and some of the people all the time, but you cannot fool all the people all the time," as perhaps Lincoln once said.[8]

Thus, even if there is no widespread challenge to the hegemony of democracy as the banner of liberty and equality, the crisis entails 'representative democracy,' namely that classification of a 'government of the people' that – according to its minimalist model – hinges both on elections by the people (as a basis of the government) and agents of the people (as actors of government). Liberals, conservatives and Marxists share the point of view that representation is waning under the burden of governmental overload and, above all, political mistrust, even though many still believe that the crisis depends on short-term or circumstantial factors.[9]

If representative democracy seems exhausted, political scientists have detected a variety of frontal attacks on governmental effectiveness and, thus, to democracy itself. Moreover, they have proposed different solutions, depending on the diagnosis. On the one hand, according to the conservative approach, the main causes of the democratic crisis are the following: delegitimisation of political authority, disaggregation of interests, governmental inadequacy in meeting rising expectations and over-participation.[10] The leftist approach, on the other hand, considers the main threats to the stability and quality of our democracy to be both the divergent system imperatives embedded in a capitalist economy and the social welfare expectations of citizens. For instance, Habermas highlights four different types of crises as a sequence of steps towards the breakdown of democracy; firstly concerning the economy, then the political-administrative system, then core institutions and, finally, the individuals and their work ethics.[11]

While there remains contention over the causes and effects, there is almost total consensus on the outcomes of the crisis,[12] no matter what conception of democracy – minimalist, medium, maximalist – is at stake: political disaffection and informal participation, declining trust in representatives, high expectations and high inadequacy, loss of popular sovereignty.

What is increasingly evident is that citizens are becoming reluctant voters – that is to say, they are denying their basic political role.[13] What is more, citizens are deserting political parties[14] and the latter, seeking to retain the illusion of being an unreplaceable point of mediation between citizens and the institutions of governance, are forced to seek financial support elsewhere, particularly from corporations and private supporters.[15] Thus the crisis of 'representative democracy' overlaps significantly with the failure of ballots and party membership. Yet one of the main – if paradoxical – virtues of our representative democracy, generally intended as the government of the people,[16] is that it hardly needs the people: it remains a fact that the percentage of citizens turning up to vote does not affect the survival of the system. Democracies are not going to collapse, even if citizens are less inclined to make the trip to the ballot box and to become a party member given that the current world seems to be far from entering a phase of real indifference: demonstrations and activism against representatives who have created suspicion, disdain or discord flourish in the streets and on the Internet as instances of so-called counter-democracy.[17]

Secondly, the persistent pursuit of both equality and individualism leads to the erosion of citizens' confidence in political leaders and institutions. Survey after survey shows that citizens hold politicians in almost complete contempt: some of the great political successes of the last decade or so, the Tea Party, the Five Stars Movement, the United Kingdom Independence Party, and Podemos, are led by figures who take advantage of the general populace's contempt for incumbents. Several counter-democratic and anti-establishment activities have, therefore, flourished as essentially preventive and oppositional.[18] Even if the contemporary notion that a people can function as an actor or agent in its own fortunes was always more a myth than a reality, in the last few decades, in those constitutional systems where the sovereignty of the people has inevitably been replaced by the 'sovereignty of the parliament,' the 'aristocratic' nature of elections and assemblies has been completely unveiled.[19] The demand for more authentic public participation, together with the increasing gulf between legitimacy and trust, is definitely a side effect of the crisis of democracy.

A further reason for the current crisis is the limited capacity for action by the government, which is unable to sustain the growing and spreading of individual demands. The result is governmental overload, and as such, an increasing crisis of trust between the people and their elected body of power. In contention with the approach followed by the American New Deal, the conservative-minimalist-elitist understanding of democracy supports a 'lean state' returning to its 'core competencies.'[20] Accordingly, due to institutional differentiation in government and in answer to the increasing needs of the citizenry, a variety of governmental tasks, from executive functions to regulatory or advisory responsibilities, have been taken over and carried out by agencies (i.e. non-majoritarian institutions or, more simply, unelected bodies) that worked far from the main institutions of democratic legitimation. This move has constituted a new branch called – erroneously but evocatively – the 'new ephorate.' (For instance, examples such as the Consob, which is the authority responsible for regulating the Stock Exchange, the Agcom, the authority with regulatory and supervisory powers in the field of communication in Italy; and service providers such as the BBC in the UK).[21]

Finally, the concept, or myth, of sovereignty plays an important role in highlighting the crisis of representative democracy. Much has been written about the real impact of globalisation, and the advance of both supranational and transnational law on the integrity of the nation state and the sovereignty of the people.[22] The reality is, on the one hand, that states rely increasingly on regional alliances, blocs and coalitions, all of which undermine the traditional role of the sovereign icon; on the other hand, the unprecedented growth of international trades and capital, in the context of a global arena, has sidelined some aspects of state sovereignty through institutional policy constraints and limitations on the ability to interfere within domestic markets. Even if rules and institutions fostered by economic globalisation, including the Organisation for Economic Co-operation and Development and the World Trade Organization, are bound to nation states for their power and their legitimacy, it is undeniable that the idea of a self-governing community is fading rapidly: the fortune of ordinary citizens depends less on the decisions of national politicians and more on the decisions of transnational corporations, money markets, derivatives traders, international agencies, supranational political entities and so on. The privatisation of law indicates the (relative) loss of state sovereignty.[23]

1.3 In quest of alternative models

The fall of the Soviet regime and the end of the division of the Western world into two opposing factions almost 30 years ago seemed to herald a global and undisputable acknowledgement of democracy. Nevertheless, constitutional law-based states[24] have continued to experience – as we have already seen – an ever-growing 'crisis.'[25] Throughout the 20th century, the traditional model of Western constitutionalism, the so-called English or Gothic model, had already started showing signs of weakness. On the one hand, European democracies have attested to an increasingly recurrent and widespread mixture of legislative and executive functions.[26] On the other hand, as previously stressed, a number of governmental activities have been taken over and carried out by private agencies. Consequently, if the separation of powers appears an extremely outdated doctrine, the theory of the mixed constitution – implying, in the first instance, synergy and concurrence rather than division among the governmental branches – qualifies as a conceptual construction, providing a more accurate depiction of the structures and functions of modern democracies.[27] Moreover, especially within the last few decades – after the discovery of the 'aristocratic' nature of election and assemblies and, therefore, of the legal fiction of the parliament as 'the mirror of the people'– 'representative democracies' have been under attack on many fronts. This can be explained in view of the need for a more authentic participation and in contrast to the gulf between legitimacy and trust in those constitutional systems where 'sovereignty of the people' is inexorably replaced by the sovereignty of the parliament, as pointed out by one of the most eminent authorities in the studies of constitutional law.[28]

The rising loss of confidence in political leaders and institutions by the citizens (i.e. the failure of the minimalist democratic model advocated by the 'elitists')[29] at a sociological and empirical level, impacts the formal idea of popular sovereignty as the right of citizens to vote and to choose their own representatives. This has encouraged the search for alternative models, which are able to promote new forms of participatory democracy.[30] Given that citizens mistrust the institutionalised powers – often considering the government to be either a useless friend or a dangerous foe – people prefer to exercise *en masse*, rather than individually, a permanent form of control and restraint over the elite.[31] In other words, after recognising that the sanctity of the ballot box is, *per se,* an unsatisfactory device, as it cannot make elected representatives honour their promises, the public, in their quest for their lost sovereignty, have consistently demanded new constitutional instruments in order to oversee and limit public powers. If, theoretically, 'imperative mandate' is a means of binding the representative to the instructions issued by the constituent, it is equally true that, in practice, this idea does not fit an open parliamentary debate. Thus there is a growing need for alternative forms of 'counter-powers' that can apply pressure to the 'elected political elite' and, accordingly, create a strong 'counter-democracy.'[32] Moreover, in the theoretical framework of 'direct democracy,' its supporters believe that new technology will pave the way for a return to an authentically participatory democracy.[33] On the contrary, opponents of opinion polls and referenda are persuaded that ochlocracy, that is the debased form of democracy according to Polybios, is the unpleasant outcome of a system in which the people – without specialised knowledge and skills – are allowed to decide issues affecting the public, either directly, that is by universal vote, or indirectly, by opinion polls, thereby inducing the political elite to do what the majority wants.[34]

1.4 From Montesquieu to *The Federalist Papers*

It is a widely held belief that any concentration of governmental power ultimately leads to arbitrary oppression, and this can result in either the violation or complete annihilation of individual liberty, depending on the circumstances.[35] Such liberal distrust of power has frequently been theorised and commented upon in both modern and ancient contexts. It has often been held that power must be limited and constrained to prevent individuals from being abused by any public authority. In line with the canonical view advanced in the 18th century by the baron of Montesquieu,[36] the division of institution-alised power into a plurality of branches and functions seems to have been the most obvious key to fixing the boundaries of governmental power and, accordingly, preventing the government from making threats in addition to safeguarding against violations of citizens' rights and liberty.[37]

'Separation of powers,' alongside the so-called technique of repre-sentation,[38] is considered one of the fundamental doctrines of mod-ern and contemporary democracy; therefore, its absence has commonly been seen in terms of militant, if not tyrannical,[39] power exercised by an absolute ruler.[40] This doctrine, in its purest form, consists of two basic and interrelated principles, which Montesquieu openly drew from the contemporary English constitution.[41]

This can be seen in two specific features of Montesquieu's text. First, a given function of the sovereign power is carried out by one of the three branches of government. Each branch cannot trespass into the area of responsibility of the two other branches; second, if a given public officer has a position in one of the three branches, he or she is forbidden to occupy any other position in any other branch at the same time. Yet in the 17th and 18th centuries, contrary to Montesquieu's assumption, England was usually, and more properly, described as a 'mixed constitution,'[42] which more closely mirrored Polybios's constitutional thought, as opposed to Aristotle's socio-political accounts.[43] In the interplay of various formal legal powers, Polybios, by exalting the constitutional equilibrium of the Roman republic, maintains that the (sovereign) power has to be divided in order to prevent any abuse of power and to shield the liberty of individuals; however, each branch of power, being an ideal portrait of one basic type of government (that is, respectively, monarchy, aristocracy, democracy), does not only have one function since the same task could be shared by different institutions.[44]

It is worth highlighting that Montesquieu's doctrine on the separation of powers only linked to the archetype of the English constitution in an ideological sense. At the constitutional level, such doctrine was thought of as a general means to avoid the abuse of monarchical power and to protect the subjects' liberty. Yet no one intended to associate it with the utopian desire to set up a democracy, and there was no specific move to ideologically shape a 'republican constitution,' a form of constitution that in the age of Montesquieu could only be found in a few of the smaller European cities.[45]

Indeed, the final coupling of 'democracy' and 'republic,' together with the separation of powers, dates back to the early 19th century, specifically in the USA. Nowadays, such a connection does not sound strange at all, yet what we commonly term 'representative democracy' was formerly labelled a 'republic' since 'democracy' and 'representation' were two disparate concepts.[46] Indeed, from an etiological, semantic and historical point of view, it is arguably an oxymoron.

Montesquieu's theory and the Roman constitution, far more than the Athenian one, inspired the American colonists.[47] On the one hand, when writing the new constitutions for the former British colonies in the second half of the 1770s, the Founding Fathers developed, strengthened, and cemented the doctrine of the separation of powers in its purest theoretical form.[48] On the other hand, the federal constitution of 1787–1789 embodied a less pure version of the theory at stake. In accordance with this version of the constitution, the president wields the executive power, the congress the legislative, and the courts the judicial; yet, in practice, the addition of a network of 'checks and balances' makes it possible to identify a number of mutual interrelations between the three branches of power. Something similar can further be seen in the historical – rather than Montesquieuian – English constitution.[49]

In addition to the embodiment of the separation doctrine, the aforementioned conceptual shift originated from the merging of two, originally disparate, concepts: 'democracy' and 'representation.' If 'democracy' is taken to be the direct rule of the sovereign people in line with the model of the Athenian πολιτεία in the 4th and 5th centuries BC, then 'representation' comes to mean something significantly different.[50] Far from being the core of any Anglo-Saxon tradition of democracy or republic,[51] representation is historically rooted in the 'parliamentary experience,' inaugurated in 1295 by Edward I, and is inextricably linked with the rule of an elite class.[52] Indeed, the English parliament (i.e. a forum where the council, as the co-ordinating agent of the king's government, controlled the agenda) emerged in the 13th century as an instrument of royal government and not as an opposing body to the Crown, which promoted liberty. In fact, the Commons were formed in order to be summoned only to consent to decisions, not to contribute to them. In other words, parliamentary representation, although masked as a republican and democratic principle by the American Founding Fathers, was just "an incident of feudal service" and not "an expression of democratic principle" or even of popular sovereignty.[53] Since the introduction of the so-called Model Parliament, the representatives were vested in *plena potestas* and, even though each representative theoretically had to act on behalf of the 'people as a whole,'[54] the constituents were bound by the representatives' free will and power.[55] This represents an overturn of the ordinary terms of Roman *mandatum*,[56] as well as a mystification of the sovereignty of the represented,[57] through the 'canon law' associated with the *persona ficta vel repraesentata*.[58]

Intentionally manipulating a number of heterogenous elements, the Founding Fathers have sought to frame the US constitution as a modern federal republic, governed as a form of representative democracy, which acted upon the new altered meaning of power flowing from the people rather than power exercised by the people.[59] The Greek πόλεις, as an example of pure democracy, showed some intrinsic and avoidable flaws, particularly since they accepted "no cure for the mischiefs of faction."[60] Accordingly, the architects of the US constitution, by applying principles "now well understood, which were either not known at all, or imperfectly known to the ancients," intended to create a new type of republic that could guarantee peace and stability and could work as "a barrier against domestic faction and insurrection."[61] The Founding Fathers made use of Montesquieu's paradigm as a direct source of inspiration concerning the doctrine of the functional division of sovereign power into separate functions and departments. Additionally, they also took advantage of the mixed constitution, which had gradually flourished in England, with regard to the traditional approach to parliamentary representation, as well as the corrective network of 'checks and balances.'[62] First, the principle of representation – unknown in ancient democracies and emphasised by Montesquieu himself in a monarchical context[63] – transformed human passions into reasoned deliberations and empowered the government to control the governed; second, the adoption of institutional checks and balances as a corrective of the separation theory, in view of constitutional equilibrium, both assumed a powerful executive branch with a strong role in the social life of citizens and the power to veto laws passed by the legislative branch.[64]

This, indeed, permitted the republican government to control itself.[65] Yet is this what Benjamin Constant referred to as a "good constitution" – that is to say, an "act of mistrust"?[66]

Notes

1 Since the late 1960s, Ursula Le Guin has insisted that science fiction is not concerned with the future but rather it is a reflection of the present; it is not predictive but rather descriptive. Similarly, in the 2000s, William Gibson, the pioneer of cyberpunk literature, moved away from the future, setting his last novels in the present-day. This explicitly allegorical use of setting, thus, opened up the genre as a means to record and reflect upon the historical moment (Le Guin 1979: 156; cf. Evans et alii 2006).
2 Thatcher 1987.
3 These are the titles of the *American Political Science Association Annual Conference* held in 2012 and the *UK Political Studies Association Annual Conference* held in 2013. See, also, Whiteley 2011.
4 For instance, some scholars suggested that ancient democracy, in the aftermath of the collapse of the Union of Soviet Socialist Republics (USSR), might replace socialism as the main political and theoretical interlocutor of Western democracies: cf. Euben - Wallach - Ober 1994. Others share the view that the history of Athenian democracy should be seen, at least, as a stimulating case study: cf. Urbinati 2002: 54 ff.;

Fontana 2004: 27 ff.; Saxonhouse 2004: 57 ff. Cf. Fishkin 1991: 81 ff.; Fishkin 1997: 18 ff.; 54 f.; 80 f.; 169; Fishkin 2001. This author is a fervent proponent of deliberative participation and – on the grounds of the Athenian experience – promotes a model focussed on consultative, rather than decision making, panels of citizens. Conversely, Samons 2004 presents a fierce attack on democracies: the author believes that the practice of both ancient Athenian and modern American democracy poses a threat to public virtue; cf. Farrar 2007: 176.

 5 See Crouch 2004; Crouch 2011; cf., moreover, Rancière 2006; Keane 2009; Della Porta 2013.
 6 Merkel 2018.
 7 Norris 2011: 241.
 8 Cf. Boller Jr. - George 1990: 88.
 9 Flinders 2012; Hay 2007.
10 Crozier - Huntington - Watanuki 1975.
11 Habermas 1973; Offe 1972.
12 Offe 1979.
13 Dalton 2004.
14 See Urbinati 2015. According to this scholar, the plebiscitarian impulse helped by mass media, the decline of traditional parties and the rise of charismatic authorities would lead to a revolt against intermediary institutions.
15 Van Biezen - Mair - Poguntke 2012.
16 Lijphart 1984: 1: "The literal meaning of democracy – government by the people – is probably also the most basic and most widely used definition."
17 See Rosanvallon 2008: *passim*.
18 The Italian "Sardines' movement" is a singular case to study. Dubbed so due to their ability to 'pack squares,' they embody a general repugnance for Salvini's anti-migrant and anti-European language and rhetoric. It is noteworthy that while Occupy, UK Uncut, 38 Degrees, Indignados and The Rules seek to pose serious challenges to the hegemonic powers, the Italian movement is not antagonistic towards the established power but – oddly – towards the opposition party. Is it a form of counter-counter-democracy? Moreover, an unconscious oligarchical element clearly emerges from the discourse of the Sardines, particularly when they resort to the old and tired formula "speaking to the head" instead of "speaking to the belly," which betrays the desire to see those people relegated to indifference and passivity, not more informed and aware.
19 On the diarchic nature of representative democracies (implying a distinction between "will" and "opinion"), see Urbinati 2006. Today, elections are regarded as the best (if not the only) way to realise democracy – that is, the spread of democracy is commonly understood as the expansion of opportunities to vote, and elections are seen as "the institutional centrepiece of modern democracy" (*contra* the so-called election fixation, see McCormick 2011: 2; 171; cf. Van Reybrouck 2016), yet the ancient Greeks considered a government grounded in elections 'aristocratic,' and the only authentic democratic mode of selection was the lot (Arist. *Pol.* 1294b7–10). The 'aristocratic' character of representative democracy had already been emphasised by Jefferson 1997: 187 (letter to John Adams,

The need for new paradigms   25

28 October 1813) and Hamilton - Jay - Madison 1987: no. 109 (Madison); see Urbinati 2006: 7; 15; 53; cf. Pitkin 1967: 193 f. On the contrary, Adams 1865: 203 ff.; 205, states that the parliament "should be an exact portrait, in miniature, of the people at large, as it should think, feel, reason and act like them." Concerning this 'descriptive representation,' see Pitkin 1967: 250: according to this author, the etymological development of the verb 'to represent' in the 17th century is complicated, but the available evidence would suggest that "terms like 'represent' were first applied to the parliament as an image of the whole nation" and that Hobbes was one of the first to use the terms 'represent' and 'representative' in a larger sense, even if, more precisely, "the earliest application...of the noun 'representative' to a member of parliament occurs in 1651," being "the year in which Hobbes published the Leviathan, in the midst of this etymological development." See Schmitt 2003: 217; 292 ff.; 305; cf. Manin - Przeworski - Stokes 1999a; Manin - Przeworski - Stokes 1999b: 31.

20 The Trilateral Report of 1975 maintains that a stable democracy – in which moderate participation is a substantial requisite – should be free from excessive expectations and from an excessive number of economic and welfare responsibilities of the state.

21 Loughlin 2010: 449 ff.; Roberts 2011.

22 Scholte 2008; Hay 2014; McGrew 2016.

23 By this I mean from the law to contracts between individuals, even if the latter are multinational companies; from the *lex* to the *lex mercatoria*.

24 That is, those shaped within the context of the rigid constitutions of the post-World War II era but substantially grounded in principles and values enucleated under the auspices of the Enlightenment.

25 See Ferrajoli 2005.

26 For instance, when by a vote of no confidence the parliament exercises the power to make the government resign or call for an election, and the government is thereby accountable to the parliament, Montesquieu's doctrine is clearly infringed as the legislative power encroaches on the executive. Likewise, a breach of the separation occurs if the government has the right to dissolve the parliament and call for an election and if the prime minister and/or the ministers (heads of the executive branch) are, at the same time, members of the parliament. It is a further breach of the separation of powers (being the role of the parliament restricted to approving or rejecting governmental proposals) if a law is drafted and initiated by the government itself. What is more, the executive is vested with a legislative power in character when laws take the form of a mere framework, whereas subsidiary regulations passed by the government (by means of the so-called *Erlasse*, *decreti legge*, statutory instruments) lay down fundamental and substantial details. See Marshall 1971: 96 ff.; Gallagher - Laver - Mair 2006: 35.

27 See Hansen 2010.

28 Mortati 1975: 23 and 36: "nessuna delle condizioni necessarie a consentire l'esercizio popolare della sovranità (pure solennemente affermato dall'art. 1 della Costituzione: La sovranità appartiene al popolo ...), si realizza in Italia" so that "il regime di poliarchia effettivamente vigente viene a realizzare una forma di sovranità del Parlamento." See Manin 1997: 134 ff.; 155 f.; 236; 238: "Representative government...is

a perplexing phenomenon…Conceived in explicit opposition to democracy, today it is seen as one of its forms"; cf. Lobrano 2006 and Lobrano - Onida 2016: esp. § 1.1; cf., moreover, Fraenkel 1958: 6 ff.; Eulau 1978: 32; Fisichella 1983: 5; Rescigno 1991: 94. Ackerman's trilogy (1991, 1998, 2014) is one of the most important contributions for supporting a return to an authentically popular sovereignty; see, moreover, Fishkin 1991 and Fishkin 1997.

29 Cf. Schumpeter 1942.

30 McCormick 2011; McCormick 2017; on the 'non-domination' principle, see Pettit 1999. Among the advocates of the so-called participatory or strong democracy, see Pateman 1970 and Barber 1984.

31 The last Standard Eurobarometers (Public Opinion in the European Union) present a grim scenario (https://ec.europa.eu/commfrontoffice/publicopinion/index.cfm/Survey/index#p=1&instruments=STANDARD). The Standard Eurobarometer 88 survey report (carried out between 5 and 19 November 2017) is a significant source, attesting to an unsurprising, yet disappointing, state of public opinion within the EU about trust in political institutions and political parties, as well as satisfaction with democracy. Only a minority of respondents trust their national government (36% versus 59%), while distrust is up by two percentage points since spring 2017 (trust has lost one point). A minority of respondents also trust the national parliament, with a slight fall (35%, –1, versus 58%, +1). Trust in political parties, very much a minority view, has also fallen by one point (18%, –1, versus 77%, +2). Forty-two percent of Europeans (unchanged since spring 2017) are dissatisfied with the way democracy works in their country (a slightly higher percentage than in 2004), but it is remarkable that respondents in ten member states remain predominantly dissatisfied with the way democracy works on a national level, most markedly in Greece (77%), Croatia (72%), Lithuania and Romania (64% in both countries) and Italy (61%). From the Standard Eurobarometer 90 survey report (carried out between 8 and 22 November 2018), it emerges that 57% of Europeans (with no change since spring 2018) are satisfied with how democracy works in their country, whereas 41% are dissatisfied: yet if satisfaction is most widespread in the Nordic countries (91% in Denmark, 81% in Finland and Sweden), in the Benelux countries (82% in Luxembourg and the Netherlands, 72% in Belgium), Austria (80%), Ireland (79%) and Germany (73%), dissatisfaction is predominant in ten member states, led by Greece (74%), Croatia (64%), Romania (63%) and Lithuania (62%): the gap consists in 65 percentage points between Denmark, where satisfaction is highest, and Greece, where it is lowest. Trust in the national government still represents the minority position, even if it has risen by one percentage point since spring 2018 (35%, +1 percentage point, against 59% distrust, –2). The same movement concerns trust in the national parliament (35%, +1, against 58% distrust, –2), while trust in political parties has fallen by one percentage point (to 18%, against 77% distrust).

32 Cf. Rosanvallon 2008: *passim.*

33 Cf. Coleman 2017.

34 See, for instance, Bilancia 2017 and Ruggeri 2018: 606 f. Yet the dilemma facing representative government is that those who can meet the

aspirations of the people by way of their specialised knowledge are also those most inclined to undermine the majority rule (see Michels 1915: 83 f.; Pitkin 1967: 135 f.). In truth, as Bobbio 1978: 32 has pointed out, direct democracy and representation "non sono due sistemi alternativi, nel senso che laddove c'è l'una non ci può essere l'altra ma sono due sistemi che possono integrarsi a vicenda."

35 Cf. Dalberg-Acton 1988: 519: "Power tends to corrupt and absolute power corrupts absolutely." He echoes the dictum pronounced by William Pitt the Elder before the UK House of Lords, after Lord Chatham, about 100 years earlier: "Unlimited power is apt to corrupt the minds of those who possess it; and this I know, my Lords, that where law ends, there tyranny begins" (Cobbett 1813: 195). Montesquieu 1748: 11.4 made a similar observation: "c'est une expérience éternelle que tout homme qui a du pouvoir est porté à en abuser." See, among the ancient authors, Plat. *Leg.* 713c; Hdt. 3.80.1–2.

36 Cf. *Révolution Française* (s.v. *Constitution*) 1802: 81.

37 Montesquieu 1748: 11.6: "Lorsque dans la même personne ou dans le même corps de magistrature, la puissance législative est réunie à la puissance exécutrice, il n'yapoint de liberté…Il n'y a point encore de liberté si la puissance de juger n'est pas séparée de la puissance législative et de l'exécutrice."

38 See, in these terms, Loewenstein 1957 (Part One, 2, § *Shared Powers and the Technique of Representation*).

39 Hamilton - Jay - Madison 1987: no. 47 (Madison): "The accumulation of all powers, legislative, executive, and judiciary, in the same hands, whether of one, a few, or many, and whether hereditary, self-appointed, or elective, may justly be pronounced the very definition of tyranny."

40 Article 16 of the *French Declaration of Human Rights* of 1789 lays down that "toute société dans laquelle la garantie des droits n'est pas assurée, ni la séparation des pouvoirs déterminée, n'a point de constitution." See the Montesquieuan model in Montesquieu 1748: 11.6: "Il y a dans chaque État trois sortes de pouvoirs…Il n'y a point…de liberté si la puissance de juger n'est pas séparée de la puissance législative et de l'exécutrice…Tout serait perdu, si le même homme, ou le même corps des principaux, ou des nobles, ou du peuple, exerçaient ces trois pouvoirs."

41 According to Montesquieu, the English constitution in force in 1748 exemplified the doctrine of the separation of powers expounded in the sixth chapter of the eleventh book, whose title was *"De la constitution d'Angleterre"*: "Il y a aussi une nation dans le monde qui a pour objet direct de sa constitution la liberté politique. Nous allons examiner les principes sur lesquels elle la fonde. S'ils sont bons, la liberté y paraîtra comme dans un miroir. Pour découvrir la liberté politique dans la constitution, il ne faut pas tant de peine. Si on peut la voir où elle est, si on l'a trouvée, pourquoi la chercher?" (Montesquieu 1748: 11.5). On the principle of the division of powers before Montesquieu, see Gwyn 1965.

42 Montesquieu's doctrine (in short: the executive power rests with the king, the legislative with the parliament and the judicial with the courts) was inspired by, or rather loosely based on, the English constitution. His 'English constitution' was more of an ideal model since the actual constitution failed to fulfil the two fundamental principles of his doctrine: the

king was the monarchical element, the House of Lords the aristocratic and the House of Commons the democratic. Sovereign power was connected to the legislature (which was divided between the 'king,' the 'House of Lords' and the 'House of Commons' since the power to pass laws was divided between two chambers, and – what is more – the king had the power to veto any law, even those passed by the parliament). Judicial power was shared by the courts, the House of Lords (which functioned as the highest court of appeal) and the king (who had the prerogative of mercy). Compare, on the fusion of the executive and legislative powers (within the frame of the British parliamentary system), Vile 1967: 13 ff.; 84 f.; Lieberman 2006. On the issue of the division of sovereign power and its relation to the theory of the mixed constitution, see Franklin 1991 and Pettit 2013.

43 The theory finds its classic formulation in Aristotle. At first, the philosopher, from a theoretical point of view, shapes a sixfold schema of ideal types of constitutions based, on the one hand, on the number of rulers (the one, the few and the many), and, on the other hand, on a positive and negative variant of each of the three types (monarchy/tyranny, aristocracy/oligarchy, πολιτεία/democracy): Arist. *Pol.* 1279a22–80a6. Later, at a more historical level of description, Aristotle replaces his sixfold schema with a new model. He rules out monarchy and tyranny since the rule of the one was almost absent in classical Greece; accordingly, he focusses only on the rule of the few and on the rule of the many and points out that oligarchy and democracy currently represent the two most common types of constitutions; then he divides each of these two types into four graduated variants, the first being the best and the fourth the worst; finally, he maintains that in a given constitution, there can be a mixture of democracy and oligarchy and uses the terms πολιτεία and ἀριστοκρατία to label two kinds of "mixed constitution," the former when the government is predominantly democratic, the latter when the oligarchic elements prevail. See Arist. *Pol.* 1286b1–52, 1289a8–11; 1290a13–29;1291b7–13; 1291b15–18; 1292b22–1293a10; 1293a10–34; 1293b31–38; 1294b14–16; 1296a22–23; 1295a25–1296b12; 1298a10–34; 1298a34–b5; 1301b39–40; 1316b39–1317a10; 1318b6–1319b32; 1320b17–1321a4; cf. de Romilly 1959; Aalders 1968 54 ff.; Nippel 1980: 52 ff.; Hansen 1993. An alternative more influential scheme of mixed constitution is found in Polybios: the Greek historian described and praised the emergence and growth of the Roman empire, taking its republican constitution as a reference point: whereas Aristotle's mixed constitution results in a mixture of two debased types of constitutions, Polybios mixes the three basic types according to their good forms: kingship, aristocracy and democracy (Polyb. 6.3.4–6, about the mixed constitution in general; 6.10.1–11, on Sparta; 6.11.11-18.9, on Rome): see, along with the aforementioned authors, Millar 2002: 23 ff.; Tatum 2009.

44 See Montesquieu 1748: 11.14: "À Rome, le peuple ayant la plus grande partie de la puissance législative, une partie de la puissance exécutrice, et une partie de la puissance de juger, c'était un grand pouvoir qu'il fallait balancer par un autre…Ils choquèrent donc la liberté de la constitution, pour favoriser la liberté du citoyen; mais celle-ci se perdit avec celle-là."

Cf. Catalano 1974 (considering Polybios's analysis an aristocratic view, shared by Cicero, opposing the popular thought emerging from Cato and Sallustius); Nicolet 1983 (emphasising the aristocratic character of the Roman republic).

45 Democracies and Republics were forms of constitutions known mainly from the past, whereas the most important states in the 18th century were monarchies. Accordingly, Montesquieu, together with his contemporary statesmen and philosophers, erroneously thought that this situation would continue in the future: on the contrary, less than half a century later, two major states – the USA and France – had adopted a republican constitution grounded on the doctrine of the separation of power.

46 The final connection among democracy, republic and separation of powers dates to the first decades of the 19th century and takes place in the USA, a federal republic governed as a 'representative democracy': for instance, the first edition of *Encyclopædia Britannica*[1] (s.v. *Democracy*) 1771: 415 defines democracy as "the same with a popular government, wherein the supreme power is lodged in the hands of the people" and emphasises that "such were Rome and Athens; but as to our modern republics, Basil only excepted, their government comes nearer to aristocracy than democracy." One of the first appearances of the new coupling of 'representation' and 'democracy' occurs in a letter from Alexander Hamilton written in 1777, but the notion of representation took decades to be definitely 'ingrafted' upon that of democracy (if one uses Paine's famous words). This semantic shift clearly emerges from the development of the name of one of the two major US parties: in 1791, James Madison and Thomas Jefferson founded the *Republican Party*; then, it was called *Democratic-Republican Party of the Nation*, and in 1828, under Andrew Jackson, it was re-labelled *Democratic Party*: Roper 1989: 54 f.; Dahl 1989: 199. In the wake of Tocqueville's *De la démocratie en Amérique*, published in 1835–1840, the new idea of democracy was rapidly connected with the concept of representation, and in 1842 – before the abolition of slavery – the seventh edition of the *Encyclopædia Britannica* (s.v. *Democracy*) 1842: 708 praised "the United States of North America at the present day" as "the most perfect example of democracy." Even if as late as 1848, the new Swiss federation still conceived of democracy and representation as direct opposites. From the middle of the 19th century the simple term 'democracy' was taken to mean 'government of representatives of the people' or 'indirect government of the people,' whereas 'pure democracy' – that is, the direct rule of the people – was downgraded to historical footnotes and utopian projects. See Hansen 2005: 5 ff.; 45 ff.

47 Reinhold 1979.

48 Hamilton - Jay - Madison 1987: no 47: Madison refers to "the celebrated Montesquieu" as "the oracle who is always consulted and cited on this subject." The Pennsylvanian constitution, for example, provided a unicameral legislative power performed by representatives of the people, as well as a Supreme Executive Council composed of 12 councillors elected by the people. On the contrary, the president and the vice-president were elected by the members of the legislative assembly and of the Supreme Executive Council from among the 12 members of the council. No

member of the assembly was permitted to have a seat on the council; the legislative and the executive had no power to control one another since a Council of Censors elected every seven years was the only governmental body in charge of evaluating whether the aforementioned branches had performed their duties.

49 As far as the federal constitution is concerned, the legislative power is divided into two chambers: The President has the power to veto laws passed by Congress; the President appoints the secretaries, but the Senate has the power to confirm or deny the nominations. The President has the power to conclude treaties with foreign powers, but treaties are subject to ratification by the Senate. Congress declares war, although this function is part of the executive power. Moreover, since 1803, the Supreme Court has been in charge of judicial review of laws, thus intruding into the Congress's power to pass laws. See Manin 2006: 27 ff.; cf. Casper 1997.

50 See Manin 1997: 1: "Contemporary democratic governments have evolved from a political system that was conceived by its founders as opposed to democracy...what today we call representative democracy has its origins (established in the wake of the English, American and French revolutions) that was in no way initially perceived as a form of democracy or of government by the people"; also, according to Schmitt 2003: 204 ff.; 228 (who echoes Rousseau), representation denies the democratic principle of "self-identity" of the people as a "political unity." On the imprecise concept involved in the term 'indirect democracy' since representation is "ingrafted upon the concept of democracy" (as Thomas Paine wrote in 1792: cf. Paine 1989: 170), see, paradigmatically, Duso 2001; cf. Morel 2000. On such divides, see Sieyès 1789: 35.

51 See Sayles 1975 (ch. 1).

52 Stephenson 1954.

53 Loughlin 2010: 248.

54 This universality is associated with the idea that in questions affecting the common law (that is, the law of the community), representatives of all communities and all people have to be involved; this claim is epitomised in a private Roman law *regula* (C. 5.59.5.2: *quod omnes similiter tangit ab omnibus comprobari debet*) that was transformed into a principle of public law – i.e. *quod omnes tangit, ab omnibus comprobetur* (Post 1964b; Bettetini 1999). See, moreover, Cam 1970: 263–279; esp. 272: "The burgesses summoned to the council of 1268 had to bring with them letters from their community declaring that they would hold as accepted and established whatever these men should do on their behalf." According to Cam, moreover, "The conception that all England was represented in the House of Commons" goes back to the Tudor times, when it was accepted that "a man was there not only for his locality but for some-thing much more; he was a publick, a Councellor to the whole State." The idea that all the people were represented in the House of Commons was then supported by Smith and Coke and further developed by Hobbes (cf. Lobrano 2012: 39 ff.; esp. 57 f.).

55 *Cum plena potestate pro se et tota communitate comitatus praedicti ad consulendum et consentiendum pro se et communitate illa.* See Post 1964a; Stubbs 1913: 76; Morris 1933: 141 ff.; 145; Edwards 1934: 141 ff.; Müller 1966: 67 ff.; Harriss 1981: 38; Guérin-Bargues 2016: 257, n. 56 f.

56 Cf. Lobrano - Onida 2016: § I.1.d.

57 Journes 1985: 44.

58 *Cum collegium in causa universitatis fingatur una persona*: Sinibaldus Fliscus 1570: c. 57.X.2.20 fo. 270ᵛ b. Cf. Thomas 2005: esp. 121 n. 21: "à partir d'Innocent IV les juristes se mirent à qualifier les communautés de "personnes fictives" (*personae fictae*), objet d'une pure représentation mentale (*repraesentatae*) ou imaginaires (*imaginariae*)"; "Le lien entre representation et fiction apparaît bien dans l'association *repraesentata et ficta*…"Personne representative et imaginaire" fut forgé par Jean XXII, dans sa décrétale sur les frères mineurs: Extrav. Joh. XXII, c. 5, 14 (*"non vera, sed repraesentata et imaginaria"*)."

59 Hamilton - Jay - Madison 1987: no. 10 (Madison): "A republic, by which I mean a government in which the scheme of representation opens a different prospect and promises the cure for which we are seeking"; Hamilton - Jay - Madison 1987: no. 22 (Hamilton): "The fabric of American empire ought to rest on the solid basis of the consent of the people. The streams of national power ought to flow immediately from that pure, original fountain of all legitimate authority." See, moreover, Hamilton - Jay - Madison 1987: no. 51 (Madison): "You must first enable the government to control the governed; and in the next place oblige it to control itself."

60 Hamilton - Jay - Madison 1987: no. 10 (Madison).

61 Hamilton - Jay - Madison 1987: no. 9 (Hamilton).

62 Hamilton - Jay - Madison 1987: no. 9 (Hamilton): "The regular distribution of power into distinct departments; the introduction of legislative balances and checks; the institution of courts composed of judges holding their offices during good behaviour; the representation of the people in the legislature by deputies of their own election." See Paine 1989: 167 f.; 170: "What is called a republic is not any particular form of government. It is wholly characteristic of the claim, matter or object for which government ought to be instituted, and on which it is to be employed, *res-publica*, the public affairs, or the public good. Every government that does not act on the principle of a Republic, or in other words, that does not make the *res-publica* its whole and sole object, is not a good government. Republican government is no other than government established and conducted for the interest of the public, as well individually as collectively"; "the government of America, which is wholly on the system of representation, is the only real republic in character and in practice that now exists…It is on this system that the American government is founded. It is representation ingrafted upon democracy."

63 According to Montesquieu 1748: 11.18, parliamentary state (or "gouvernement gothique") is a "gouvernement fondé sur un corps législatif formé par les représentants d'une nation," or, in other words, a government "d'abord mêlé de l'aristocratie et de la monarchie." See Magnou-Nortier 1993; Ourliac 1995.

64 Hamilton - Jay - Madison 1987: no. 71 (Hamilton). According to Montesquieu himself, "si la puissance exécutrice n'a pas le droit d'arrêter les entreprises du corps législatif, celui-ci sera despotique" (Montesquieu 1748: 11.6).

65 Cf. Mansfield Jr. 1993: 247: One of the most commendable results achieved by the American constitution would be the creation of "the first republic with a strong executive that is consistent with republicanism."
66 Constant 1992: 53.

Bibliography

G.J.D. Aalders, *Die Theorie der gemischten Verfassung im Altertum*, Amsterdam, 1968.
B. Ackerman, *We the People, Foundations*, Cambridge, 1991.
B. Ackerman, *Transformations*, Cambridge, 1998.
B. Ackerman, *The Civil Rights Revolution*, Cambridge, 2014.
J. Adams, Letter to John Penn. January 1775, in *The Works of John Adams, Second President of the United States of America*, ed. C.F. Adams, Boston, IV, 1865, 203–209.
B. Barber, *Strong Democracy: Participatory Politics for a New Age*, Berkeley, 1984.
A. Bettini, Riflessioni storico-dogmatiche sulla regola *quod omnes tangit* e la *persona ficta*, *Il diritto ecclesiastico* 110 (1999), 645–679.
P. Bilancia (ed.), *Democrazia diretta vs Democrazia rappresentativa*, *Federalismi.it* 1 (2017): https://www.federalismi.it/focus/index_focus.cfm?FOCUS_ID=75&focus=special.
N. Bobbio, Democrazia rappresentativa e democrazia diretta, in *Democrazia e partecipazione*, ed. G. Quazza, Torino, 1978, 19–46.
P.F. Boller Jr., J. George, *They Never Said It: A Book of Fake Quotes, Misquotes, and Misleading Attributions*, Oxford, 1990.
H.M. Cam, The theory and practice of representation in Medieval England, in *Historical Studies of the English Parliament*, eds. E.B. Fryde and E. Miller, Cambridge, I, *Origins to 1399*, 1970, 263–279.
G. Casper, *Separating Powers: Essays on the Founding Period*, Cambridge, 1997.
P. Catalano, La divisione del potere in Roma (a proposito di Polibio e di Catone), in *Studi in onore di G. Grosso*, Torino, VI, 1974, 665–691.
W. Cobbett, *The Parliamentary History of England from the Earliest Period to the Year 1803*, London, XVI, 1813.
S. Coleman, *Can the Internet Strengthen Democracy?*, Cambridge, 2017.
B. Constant, *Recueil d'articles 1829–1830. Texte établi, introduit, annoté et commenté par É. Harpaz*, Paris, 1992.
C. Crouch, *Post-Democracy*, Cambridge, 2004.
C. Crouch, *Das befremdliche Überleben des Neoliberalismus – Postdemokratie*, Frankfurt a.M., II, 2011.
M.J. Crozier, S. Huntington, J. Watanuki, *The Crisis of Democracy. Report on the Governability of Democracies to the Trilateral Commission*, New York, 1975.
R.A. Dahl, *Democracy and Its Critics*, New Haven/London, 1989.

J. Dalberg-Acton (Lord Acton), Letter to Bishop Mandell Creighton (3 April 1887), in *Selected Writings of Lord Acton*, ed. J.R. Fears, Indianapolis, III, *Essays in Religion, Politics and Morality*, 1988, 519.

R.J. Dalton, *Democratic Challenges, Democratic Choices: The Erosion of Political Support in Advanced Industrial Democracies*, Oxford, 2004.

J. de Romilly, Le classement des constitutions de Hérodote à Aristote, *Revue des études grecques* 72 (1959), 81–99.

D. Della Porta, *Can Democracy Be Saved? Participation, Deliberation and Social Movements*, Cambridge, 2013.

G. Duso, Pensare la democrazia: le aporie dei concetti, in *Paradosso*, eds. U. Curi and C. Sini, Padova, 2001, 83–114.

Encyclopædia Britannica[1], s.v. *Democracy*, Edinburgh, II, 1771, 415.

Encyclopædia Britannica[7], s.v. *Democracy*, Edinburgh, VII, 1842, 708.

J.G. Edwards, The *Plena Potestas* of English Parliamentary Representation, in *Oxford Essays in Medieval History presented to H.E. Salter*, ed. F.M. Powicke, Oxford, 1934, 141–154.

J.P. Euben, J.R. Wallach, J. Ober, Introduction, in *Athenian Political Thought and the Reconstruction of American Democracy*, eds. J.P. Euben, J.R. Wallach and J. Ober, Ithaca/London, 1994, 1–26.

H. Eulau, Changing Views of Representation, in *The Politics of Representation: Continuities in Theory and Research*, eds. H. Eulau and J.C. Wahlke, Beverly Hills, 1978, 31–53.

A.B. Evans et al., Editorial Introduction: The 100th Issue of SFS, *Science Fiction Studies* 33.100 (2006), 385–388.

C. Farrar, Power to the People, in *Origins of Democracy in Ancient Greece. The Invention of Politics in Classical Athens*, eds. K.A. Raaflaub, J. Ober and R.W. Wallace, Berkeley/London, 2007, 170–195.

L. Ferrajoli, The Crisis of Democracy in the Era of Globalisation, in *Anales de la Cátedra Francisco Suárez* 39 (2005), 53–67.

J.S. Fishkin, *Democracy and Deliberation: New Directions for Democratic Reform*, New Haven, 1991.

J.S. Fishkin, *The Voice of the People*, New Haven, 1997.

J.S. Fishkin, *When the People Speak*, New York, 2001.

D. Fisichella, *La rappresentanza politica*, Milano, 1983.

M. Flinders, *Defending Politics: Why Democracy Matters in the Twenty-First Century*, Oxford, 2012.

S. Fliscus (Innocentius IV), *Super libros quinque Decretalium commentaria*, Francofurti ad Moenum, 1570.

B. Fontana, Rhetoric and the Roots of Democratic Politics, in *Talking Democracy. Historical Perspectives on Rhetoric and Democracy*, eds. B. Fontana, C. Nederman and G. Remer, Pennsylvania, 2004, 27–56.

J.H. Franklin, Sovereignty and the Mixed Constitution: Bodin and His Critics, in *The Cambridge History of Political Thought 1450–1700*, eds. J.H. Burns with M. Goldie, Cambridge, 1991, 298–328.

34   *The need for new paradigms*

E. Fraenkel, *Die repräsentative und die plebiszitäre Komponente im demokratischen Verfassungsstaat*, Tübingen, 1958.

M. Gallagher, M. Laver, P. Mair, *Representative Government in Modern Europe*[4], New York, 2006,

C. Guérin-Bargues, Le Parlement de la Réforme et la naissance de l'Eglise d'Angleterre, in *Jus Politicum* 16 (2016), 247–267

W.B. Gwyn, *The Meaning of the Separation of Powers: An Analysis of the Doctrine from its Origin to the Adoption of the United States Constitution*, New Orleans, 1965.

J. Habermas, *Legitimationsprobleme im Spätkapitalismus*, Frankfurt a.M., 1973.

A. Hamilton, J. Jay, J. Madison, *The Federalist Papers*, ed. I. Kramnick, London, 1987 (1787[1]).

M.H. Hansen, Aristotle's Alternative to the Sixfold Model of Constitutions, in *Aristote et Athènes*, ed. M. Piérart, Paris, 1993, 91–101.

M.H. Hansen, *The Tradition of Ancient Greek Democracy and its Importance for Modern Democracy*, Copenhagen, 2005.

M.H. Hansen, The Mixed Constitution versus the Separation of Powers: Monarchical and Aristocratic Aspects of Modern Democracy, *History of Political Thought* 31 (2010), 509–531.

G.L. Harriss, The Formation of Parliament, 1272–1377, in *The English Parliament in the Middle Ages*, eds. R.G. Davies and J.H. Denton, Manchester, 1981, 29–60.

C. Hay, *Why We Hate Politics*, Cambridge, 2007.

C. Hay, Globalisation's Impact on States, in *Global Political Economy*, ed. J. Ravenhill, Oxford, 2014, 287–316.

T. Jefferson, *Political Writings*, Cambridge, 1997.

C. Journes, *L'État britannique*, Paris, 1985.

J. Keane, *The Life and Death of Democracy*, London, 2009.

U. Le Guin, Introduction to the Left Hand of Darkness, in *The Language of the Night: Essays on Fantasy and Science Fiction*, ed. S. Wood, New York, 1979, 155–159.

D. Lieberman, The Mixed Constitution and the Common Law, in *The Cambridge History of Eighteenth-Century Political Thought*, eds. M. Goldie and R. Wokler, Cambridge, 2006, 317–346.

A. Lijphart, *Democracies. Patterns of Majoritarian and Consensus Government in Twenty-one Countries*, New Haven, 1984.

G. Lobrano, Dottrine della 'inesistenza' della costituzione e 'modello' del diritto pubblico romano, in *Tradizione romanistica e Costituzione*, eds. L. Labruna, M.P. Baccari and C. Cascione, Napoli, I, 2006, 321–363.

G. Lobrano, Per la comprensione del pensiero costituzionale di J.-J. Rousseau e del diritto romano, in *Il principio della democrazia – Jean-Jacques Rousseau, Du Contrat social (1762). Nel 300° della nascita di Jean-Jacques Rousseau e nel 250° della pubblicazione del Contrat social. Atti del Seminario di Studi, Sassari, 20–21 settembre 2010*, Napoli, 2012, 39–71.

G. Lobrano, P.P. Onida, Rappresentanza o/e partecipazione. Formazione della volontà "per" o/e "per mezzo di" altri. Nei rapporti individuali e collettivi, di diritto privato e pubblico, romano e positivo, *Diritto@Storia* 14 (2016): http://www.dirittoestoria.it/14/contributi/Lobrano-Onida-Rappresentanza-o-e-partecipazione.htm.

K. Loewenstein, *Political Power and the Governmental Process*, Chicago, 1957.

M. Loughlin, *Foundations of Public Law*, Oxford, 2010.

E. Magnou-Nortier, Les lois féodales et la société d'après Montesquieu et M. Bloch ou la seigneurie banale reconsidérée, *Revue Historique* 586 (1993), 321–360.

B. Manin, *The Principles of Representative Government*, Cambridge, 1997.

B. Manin, Checks, Balances and Powers: The Separation of Powers in the Constitutional Debate of 1787, in *The Invention of the Modern Republic*, ed. B. Fontana, Cambridge, 2006, 27–62.

B. Manin, A. Przeworski, S.C. Stokes, Introduction, in *Democracy, Accountability, and Representation*, eds. A. Przeworski, S.C. Stokes and B. Manin, Cambridge, 1999a, 1–26.

B. Manin, A. Przeworski, S.C. Stokes, Elections and Representation, in *Democracy, Accountability, and Representation*, eds. A. Przeworski, S.C. Stokes and B. Manin, Cambridge, 1999b, 29–54.

H.C. Mansfield Jr., *Taming the Prince: The Ambivalence of Modern Executive Power*, Baltimore, 1993.

G. Marshall, *Constitutional Theory*, Oxford, 1971.

J. McCormick, *Machiavellian Democracy*, Cambridge, 2011.

J. McCormick, Rousseau's Rome and the Repudiation of Populist Republicanism, *Critical Review of International Social and Political Philosophy* 10 (2017), 3–27.

A. McGrew, The Logics of Economic Globalisation, in *Global Political Economy*[5], ed. J. Ravenhill, Oxford, 2016, 255–286.

W. Merkel, Challenge or Crisis of Democracy?, in *Democracy and Crisis: Challenges in Turbulent Times*, eds. W. Merkel and S. Kneip, Berlin, 2018, 1–28.

R. Michels, *Political Parties: A Sociological Study of the Oligarchical Tendencies of Modern Democracy*, Glencoe, 1915.

F. Millar, *The Roman Republic in Political Thought*, Boston, 2002.

Montesquieu (C.-L. de Secondat), *De l'Esprit des lois*, Geneva, 1748.

L. Morel, La démocratie directe. Problèmes et formes nouvelles: Vers une démocratie directe partisane? En relisant Ian Budge, *Revue française de science politique* 50 (2000), 765–778.

W.A. Morris, The Beginnings of the House of Commons, *Pacific Historical Review* 2 (1933), 141–157.

C. Mortati, *Commentario della Costituzione*, ed. G. Branca, Bologna, 1975 (sub Art. 1).

C. Müller, *Das imperative und freie Mandat. Überlegungen zur Lehre von der Repräsentation des Volkes*, Leiden, 1966.

C. Nicolet, Polybe et la 'constitution' de Rome: aristocratie et démocratie, in *Demokratia et Aristokratia. À propos de Caius Gracchus: mots grecs et réaltiés romaines*, ed. C. Nicolet, Paris, 1983, 5–35.

W. Nippel, *Mischverfassungstheorie und Verfassungsrealität in Antike und früher Neuzeit*, Stuttgart, 1980.

P. Norris, *Democratic Deficit: Critical Citizens Revisited*, Cambridge, 2011.

C. Offe, *Strukturprobleme des kapitalistischen Staates: Aufsätze zur Politischen Soziologie*, Frankfurt a.m., 1972.

C. Offe, Unregierbarkeit - Zur Renaissance konservativer Krisentheorien, in *Stichworte zur geistigen Situation der Zeit*, ed. J. Habermas, Frankfurt a.M, I, *Nation und Republik*, 1979, 294–318.

P. Ourliac, *Montesquieu historien de la féodalité*, in *Mélanges Vellas. Recherches et réalisations*, Paris, 1995, 437–449.

T. Paine, The Rights of Man, in *Political Writings*, ed. B. Kuklick, Cambridge, 1989, 49–203.

C. Pateman, *Participation and Democratic Theory*, Cambridge, 1970.

P. Pettit, *Republicanism: A Theory of Freedom and Government*, Oxford, 1999.

P. Pettit, Two Republican Traditions, in *Republican Democracy: Liberty, Law and Politics*, eds. A. Niederberger and P. Schink, Edinburgh, 2013, 169–204.

H.F. Pitkin, *The Concept of Representation*, Berkeley/Los Angeles, 1967.

G. Post, *Plena Potestas* and Consent in Medieval Assemblies, in *Studies in Medieval Legal Thought: Public Law and the State 1100–1322*, Princeton, 1964a, 91–162.

G. Post, A Romano-Canonical Maxim, *Quod Omnes Tangit* in Bracton and in Early Parliaments, in *Studies in Medieval Legal Thought: Public Law and the State 1100–1322*, Princeton, 1964b, 163–239.

J. Rancière, *Hatred of Democracy*, London, 2006.

M. Reinhold, Eighteenth-Century American Political Thought, in *Classical Influences on Western Thought A.D. 1650–1870*, ed. R.R. Bolgar, Cambridge, 1979, 223–243.

G.U. Rescigno, La sovranità popolare ieri e oggi, in *Principi dell'89 e Costituzione democratica*, ed. L. Carlassare, Padova, 1991, 85–96.

Révolution Française. Table alphabétique du Moniteur de 1787 jusqu'à l'an 8, de la République (1799), s.v. Constitution, Paris, VI, An X de la République Française, 1802, 81.

A. Roberts, *The Logic of Discipline. Global Capitalism and the Architecture of Government*, Oxford, 2011.

J. Roper, *Democracy and its Critics: Anglo-American Democratic Thought in the Nineteenth Century*, London, 1989.

P. Rosanvallon, *Counter-Democracy. Politics in an Age of Distrust*, trans., Cambridge, 2008.

A. Ruggeri, 'Forma di governo' e 'sistema dei partiti': due categorie ormai inservibili per la teoria costituzionale?, *Consulta online* 3 (2018), 599–615.

L.J. Samons, *What's Wrong with Democracy? From Athenian Practice to American Worship*, London/Berkeley, 2004.

A.W. Saxonhouse, Democratic Deliberation and the Historian's Trade: the Case of Thucydides, in *Talking Democracy. Historical Perspectives on Rhetoric and Democracy*, eds. B. Fontana, C. Nederman and G. Remer, Pennsylvania, 2004, 57–86.

G.O. Sayles, *The King's Parliament of England*, London, 1975.

C. Schmitt, *Verfassungslehre*[9], Berlin, 2003 (1928[1]).

J.A. Scholte, Defining Globalisation, *World Economy* 31 (2008), 1471–1502.

J.A. Schumpeter, *Capitalism, Socialism and Democracy*, New York, 1942.

E.-J. Sieyès, *Observations sur le rapport du comité de constitution, concernant la nouvelle organisation de la France*, Versailles, 1789.

C. Stephenson, The Beginnings of Representative Government in England, in *Medieval Institutions. Selected Essays*, ed. B.D. Lyon, Ithaca, 1954, 126–138.

W. Stubbs, *Select Charters and Other Illustrations of English Constitutional History from the Earliest Times of the Reign of Edward the First*[9], Oxford, 1913 (1870[1]).

W.J. Tatum, Roman Democracy?, in *Greek and Roman Political Thought*, ed. R.K. Balot, Malden, 2009, 214–227.

M. Thatcher, Interview for *Woman's Own* ("no such thing as society"), *Margaret Thatcher Foundation* (September 23, 1987): https://www.margaretthatcher.org/document/106689.

Y. Thomas, Les artifices de la vérité en droit commun médiéval, *L'Homme* 175–176 (2005), 113–130.

N. Urbinati, *Mill on Democracy. From the Athenian Polis to Representative Government*, Chicago/London, 2002.

N. Urbinati, *Representative Democracy: Principles and Genealogy*, Chicago, 2006.

N. Urbinati, A Revolt Against Intermediary Bodies, *Constellations* 22 (2015), 477–486.

P.F. Whiteley, Is the Party Over? The Decline of Party Activism and Membership across the Democratic World, *Party Politics* 16.1 (2011), 21–44.

I. Van Biezen, P. Mair, T. Poguntke, Going, Going,…Gone? The Decline of Party Membership in Contemporary Europe, *European Journal of Political Research* 51.1 (2012), 24–56.

D. Van Reybrouck, *Against Elections: The Case for Democracy*, London, 2016.

M.J.C. Vile, *Constitutionalism and the Separation of Powers*, Oxford, 1967.

2   Δημοκρατία
Back to the future

2.1 Δημοκρατία and democracy

The previous chapter focussed on two conceptual and historical flaws affecting the main dimensions within which 'constitutional democracy' is articulated. That is, the institutional separation of powers and the policy of representative democracy. This covered (1) the early monarchical background of Montesquieu's doctrine and its subsequent inception in the republican context and (2) the merging of two conflicting ideals: democracy and representation. Beyond this, as already mentioned, many practical criticisms – concerning features of the modern and contemporary world – have been raised by those who champion an authentic return to the core of democracy.

In the late 18th century, democracy was still etymologically conceived of as the direct 'κράτος of the δῆμος'[1] – that is, 'rule of the people' or 'people power.' Even if the noun δῆμος was used to embrace the 'citizen body' as a whole so that the δῆμος encapsulated at the same time both ruler and ruled,[2] this form of constitution was often perceived as either only fitting small city states or in terms of radical mob rule, which was inclined towards anarchy. As Hansen has pointed out, between late-classical antiquity and the modern era, Greek democracy was a "Sleeping Beauty" whose awakening turned out to be not so romantic as in the fable. Democracy was disdained – more than kissed – by princes, as well as detested by philosophers and often found unpalatable by statesmen.[3] Only gradually, after representation was incorporated into the democratic system, did the picture start to change in the second half of the 19th century. This marked a conceptual shift that merged *res publica* and δημοκρατία under the heading 'democracy.' Even while democracy in its purest form continued to be repudiated, during the second decade of the 20th century, President Wilson in his "War Message to Congress," uttered his famous phrase about "making the world safe for democracy." In 1915 London, busses displayed an English translation of Perikles's praise of liberty.[4] All of this laid the groundwork for further modern reception, including the notable examples of President Bush's promise "to export democracy both at home and abroad" and the use of the first lines of Perikles's description of the 5th century BC Athenian democracy as the opening to the preamble of the EU-convention's draft proposal for a European Constitution in 2003.[5] However, this reception of Perikles was later omitted.

As we have already seen, democracies currently appear to be in trouble; however, the environmental crisis may turn out to be an opportune moment in the quest for a cure for the evils affecting our systems. While these systems are floundering rather than outrightly failing, the miracles of modern technology continue to spread hope by coming back to the origins of democracy. The notion of the rediscovery and actualising of the radical model of a people truly invested in sovereign power is no longer a utopian ideal. It is often seen as unpalatable due to the long-standing belief that direct government of the people is not the best option. Yet while it may continue to be unpalatable, nowadays, it can no longer be considered technically unfeasible.

2.2 The Athenian model

Lincoln's famed Gettysburg Address, where the American constitution was applauded as "government of the people, by the people, for the people," has a chance to revive from the ashes of the current model of representative democracy and within the prosperous framework of our digital age. However, we may still see this as more of a riddle rather than a recipe.[6] Two issues remain unexamined: Who constitutes 'the people' in terms of the ruler? And who are 'the people' in the role of being ruled? In the past, Athenians – as many scholars have rightly emphasised – provided various answers to these questions.[7] Even today, given that liberals, socialists, populists, dictators, and presidents boast that they represent the will of the people, clearly, more than the ideology, it is the operational meaning of democracy which deserves a thorough investigation.

On the one hand, in the 4th century BC, Aristotle interpreted δημοκρατία in terms of rule by the common people by stressing both the role played by numerical equality, rather than proportionate equality, and the link between 'popular supremacy' and the 'bare majority.' The real sovereign was, in his opinion, the πλῆθος – i.e. the 'mass' populace as opposed to the elite but not the entire citizen body. The δῆμος, as a ruler, was a part of the populace (corresponding to the lowest classes of the πόλις), not the whole of it (corresponding to the entire πόλις – i.e. πάντες πολῖται, all citizens).[8] On the opposite side, many 5th and 4th century BC authors, both supporters and foes of democracy, tended to challenge this idea by arguing on a more practical level. In championing a sociological and numerical perspective, Aristotle erroneously mapped the Athenian δῆμος onto a limited section of society, an approach which confused the way δημοκρατία actually worked as a form of government, which gave sovereign power to the majority, with what δημοκρατία was in principle – that is, a political reality encompassing both mass and elite groups ruled by the law.[9]

In fact, the δῆμος in Athens can be approached from a number of different but complementary viewpoints, which implies a twofold political concept: I suggest the δῆμος *in actu*, that is, the people – here used as a singular noun – *exercising* the κράτος can be contrasted with the δῆμος *in potentia*, that is, the people – here used as a plural noun – *entitled to* exercise the κράτος regardless of the specific declination of κράτος (power).[10]

In the text of the *Athenaion politeia*, reluctantly but realistically, the δῆμος can be considered ὁ κρατῶν – i.e. 'the (most) powerful (entity)' within the Athenian constitutional and legal system.[11] Furthermore, the main character of Aristophanes's *Knights*, Mr Demos of Pnyx Hill (a fierce caricature of the popular ruler), is comically described as "half-deaf" (ὑπόκωφον).[12] Taking this into account, it is clear that from a linguistic point of view δῆμος is more than a singular-collective noun which takes a singular verb. Rather, it synthetically embraces a multitude of disaggregated individuals, such as in Greek, λαός (people) and στρατός (army), and in English, flock and herd. The δῆμος is, at first, a unified political entity, a corporate body, an autonomous agent conceived of as having and being able to implement its will. Undoubtedly, the δῆμος is made up of numerous, free, and equal individuals.[13] Yet as a single collective entity with corporate character, it both wills and acts. It also listens to speeches, approves and rejects proposals, makes decisions, and votes. The phrase 'δῆμος κρατεῖ' does not mean 'people *have* the power'; rather, it corresponds to the concept that 'a people *has* the power to.' However, the question remains: What is the δῆμος?

The unison and personality of the δῆμος as a unit,[14] even before equality and freedom within the δῆμος,[15] represent the main pillars on which the architectural structure of democracy rests, both as an

ideology and as a political system.[16] These pillars, at the beginning of
the 6th century BC, were instigated by Solon through his most
'demotic' reforms. "What did I leave unaccomplished of all the targets for which I brought the δῆμος together?" wonders the great lawgiver in a famous passage of his elegy.[17] Solon clearly boasts that he
has transformed the δῆμος into an authentic political body. In other
words, from a body vested with no political power,[18] if not from a
pre-constitutional mass of atomised individuals at the mercy of the
public authorities,[19] then to the Athenian 'people' as a political institution that willed and acted as a single powerful agent, alongside the
ἄρχοντες and the Areiopagos. Therefore, a counter-power was constitutionally established, replacing the previous 'oligarchic' and the
'aristocratic' elements of the mixed Athenian system.[20] Solon was not
the founder of Athenian democracy;[21] however, he paved the way for
it. Furthermore, he accomplished this within the judicial sphere, leaving untouched the legislative one. In other words, the first historical
epiphany of the people as a corporate body (originally called ἡλιαία)[22]
consisted of providing judgement and in quashing decisions made by
the ἄρχοντες. The people – including those who belonged to the lowest classes – became 'the one,' sitting as a supreme court, though not
as a lawgiver. Furthermore, the original κράτος of this body was
achieved by eroding previous judicial capacities rather than flanking
the magistrates' jurisdiction.

As a result of Solon's reforms, the Athenian people represented
itself in the political realm and established its own power by judging:
the shift from the δῆμος 'sum of individuals' to the δῆμος 'institutionalised corporate body' was the first milestone, and a fundamental
one, along the path towards the full supremacy the people gradually
achieved throughout the 5th century BC. It is no coincidence that
Solon himself is credited with the introduction of a further law
against the κατάλυσις τοῦ δήμου,[23] which can be better understood as
'the dissolution of the people' rather than 'the overthrow of democracy.'[24] If the δῆμος in the capacity of exercising its κράτος was
abolished – that is, dissolved back into a pre-constitutional mass – it
could murmur, complain, speak up, or take to the streets, but it could
not wield any power. Solon was aware that popular power was
inconceivable without a corporate body, just as a corpse possesses
neither life nor political personality.[25]

If at the beginning of the 6th century the δῆμος, as a whole, ruled
as a sort of 'second instance' judge in its role of ἡλιαία, it is also
accepted that in the 5th century, the Athenian popular assembly was

perceived of as the core of democracy, despite the fact that the council, courts, and public offices were political institutions which were democratically constituted and played important roles.[26] As "historical processes advance by incremental change and by sudden ruptures," not even democracy "was instituted, so to speak, by the stroke of a pen at any one time by any one person."[27]

Henceforth, the noun δῆμος itself was often used to indicate the popular assembly endowed with legislative powers.[28] As is well known, the common prescript ἔδοξε τῶι δήμωι, also reflected in ἔδοξε τῆι βουλῆι καὶ τῶι δήμωι, appears for the first time in an Athenian inscription of the late 6th century BC. During the 4th century BC, this became the standard formula for the most part of the extant decrees, meaning "it was decided by the council and by the assembly."[29] In this context, δῆμος is, once again, a noun that corresponds neither to 'mass' as a collective singular nor to 'people' as a plural. The ruling (κρατῶν) people, again, can be seen as a corporate body whose power reveals increasingly novel content and form. It was at the end of the 6th century BC that Kleisthenes not only enacted constitutional reforms, with the aim of promoting equality among the citizens, as well as participation in running the political system,[30] but also metaphorically "added the δῆμος to his ἑταιρεία" – i.e. to "his aristocratic fraternity" – and handed it the constitution.[31] Treating the people as a pair, the Alcmeonid leader gave the Athenian assembly unprecedented power. So as to further reduce the magisterial prerogatives, the Athenian assembly instigated voting statutes and decrees.[32] The δῆμος thus transformed into a real constitutional entity: tragedy and, at the same time, politics, together brought the Athenian people ever closer to resemble a human and collective king.[33]

Such a king did not resemble a tyrant or an Eastern despot:[34] the majesty of the democratic king, the δῆμος, was balanced by the majesty of a 'spiritual' king, the νόμος.[35] The so-called *dikastic* or *heliastic* oath makes this clear.[36] Laws were, as of the beginning of the 6th century BC, the basis of the judicial power held by the Athenian people, first sitting, as a whole, in the Solonian ἡλιαία and later divided into a multiplicity of δικαστήρια.[37] Judges were, and had to be, guardians of the law, and the judges showed disapproval by casting their ballots according to the existing laws and by punishing those who had infringed on those laws.[38] Pity, favour, benevolence, and other emotions, such as enmity, were not involved in the process or considered relevant in accomplishing judicial tasks.[39]

Similarly, in the 5th century BC, the indictment for making a proposal contrary to the nomic system in force (γραφὴ παρανόμων)[40] reveals an unbreakable bond between democracy as a system directed to implement the will of the people and the rule of law as a system directed to frame and ground the democracy itself. As it transpires, this bond turned out to be even stronger than in our current constitutional order. In Athens, new statutes passed by the δῆμος were valid and effective, so long as they were not inconsistent with, or contrary to, previous legislation. Thus, in accordance with the proviso *lex anterior derogat posteriori*, if a new enactment trumped either a previous νόμος or one of the principles on which the democratic constitution was based, the *anterior* rule would have prevailed over the *posterior* one.[41] The legal procedure of the γραφὴ παρανόμων sought to prevent this: during the discussion of a bill before the assembly, or even after it had been approved by the popular assembly, anyone who wished to could present an indictment for making a παράνομον proposal. The case was then tried before a panel of judges, which could range in size from 500 to 6,000. If the accusation was grounded, either the enactment was repealed (if the charge was brought after the vote) or the bill could not be enacted (if the charge was brought before the vote). In the case of the acquittal of the accused, the unapproved proposal was enacted. If less than one year had elapsed since the presentation of the bill, the proposer could be fined and, on the third offence, he lost his citizenship.

Not only judges, popular prosecutors, and magistrates were expected to abide by the law but also the lawgiver – as a responsible yet unaccountable 'constitutional' agent – was limited in exercising its κράτος by the majesty of the νόμοι. As the γραφή παρανόμων indirectly demonstrates,[42] democracy was the monarchy of the people; the people – except for rare, and therefore noteworthy, cases[43] – acted as an attentive and rational sovereign and did not tolerate any legal change which sought to diminish its own judicial and legislative κράτος or modify the nomic frame of its own κράτος. Just as the people power was believed to be unalterable constitutionally, the established laws were likewise believed to be unchangeable throughout the 5th century BC.

The will of the Athenian people found its final construction in the text of a compact and basically closed 'legal consolidation' only after a catastrophic decade marked by the failure of the invasion of Sicily, the naval disaster at Arginusae, two oligarchical *coups*, the defeat against the Spartans, and the anarchy and the fratricidal struggle of 403 BC. On the one hand, ancient laws were revised and republished as the 'manifesto' of the reborn democratic system, and on the other, all legal provisions previously excluded from revisions were to be considered repealed. Moreover, the people, together with its double κράτος, found in the law new recognition and protection. This was the result of a series of significant reforms which endorsed two complementary measures that rather than attempting to restrain the people's extreme power were inspired more by the following needs: increasing the role played by popular judges, preserving coherency among the laws, allowing for changes in the nomic system as a result of specific and variable needs, preventing or limiting frivolous legislative proposals, and quashing unsuitable laws.[44]

The first measure was a stringent and multi-level procedure directed to enact new laws or to modify existing ones (νομοθεσία). The second was a public legal procedure aimed at those who had not sufficiently satisfied the requirements of enactment or change (γραφὴ νόμον μὴ ἐπιτήδειον θεῖναι).[45] Thus as of 403–402 BC, alongside the new distinction between a law and a decree, the power to pass laws was given to a new popular body. The νομοθέται – that is, several hundred sworn judges convened and appointed by the assembly – would vote in the last stage of a legislative procedure that in many ways resembled a 'trial of the proposed law,' with speakers arguing for and against the proposal.[46] As for the indictment of inexpediently proposing a law, it was introduced, at first, to allow anyone who wished to prosecute the proponent of a detrimental new law – that is, a law that was considered to be of limited use to or even harmful to the Athenian people; secondly, this measure could also be used to repeal a law proposed or passed by infringing secondary rules relating to the new legislative procedure; thirdly, it was aimed at those who had proposed a new law that turned out, in light of a comparative examination, to be inconsistent with previously enacted laws which had been published in the year 403–402 BC or passed later that the defendant had failed to repeal in advance. If the popular court judged against the proposer, the law – even though pre-authorised by the council and the assembly and then approved by the νομοθέται – was annulled as μὴ ἐπιτήδειος. If the case had been brought forward within a year of being passed, the defendant was also liable to pay a penalty, which did not exclude the death penalty.[47]

Having made it clear that the δῆμος is, first and foremost, a collective, singular body that, in exercising its two main constitutional powers, judicial and legislative, resembles a king, the double meaning of this term can be seen to take shape. The word δῆμος, even when its usage includes the elite populace, remains a 'partial' concept.[48] It does not cover the Athenian population in its entirety. Even if Athens differed from those systems which required property as a qualification for political rights, the δῆμος, as lawgiver and judge, did not include those who were considered marginal for reasons of gender, race, age, freedom, or dignity. These included women, foreigners, minors, slaves, ἄτιμοι, public debtors, and male prostitutes. Thus these individuals did not have any share in the κράτος.[49] From this perspective, it is apparent that the distinction between those who rule and those who are ruled remained distinct: to this extent, modern and contemporary democracies overlap with Athenian δημοκρατία. The centrality of adult male citizens, regardless of their economic status, demonstrates the sense in which ancient Athens was democratic in relation to the modern and contemporary models. That is, by current standards, a form of oligarchy (not democracy),[50] even if it amounted to a government by the people instead of government by those elected by the people. In many respects, this is irrelevant, and what emerges is an 'amatorial' system, where common people monopolised each sector of the constitutional machine. Those who were selected to take up a post as ἀρχαί (that is, magistrates or public officers) were directly drawn from the people; however, the judicial courts and the assembly directly expressed the wishes of the people.

Yet, as we know, the δῆμος (the people as a singular-collective noun) was potentially given the κράτος. While every adult male citizen had the potential to be given a share in political rights, the question concerning the identification of the 'δῆμος *in actu*' remains. Who among the 'people' (plural noun) definitively exercised the κράτος? Who was implicated in the 'rule' of the δῆμος (i.e. the people as a singular political agent)? Setting aside the problem concerning ἄτιμοι and strangers, the Athenian assembly was theoretically open to all πολῖται, yet not all could attend, nor did all necessarily want to. The assembly's usual meeting place on the Pnyx could not hold more than 6,000–8,000 people, which roughly equates to only a fifth of the entire citizenry.[51] Those who wanted to listen, to speak, and to vote simply had to arrive as early as possible in order to find a seat and contribute to the exercising of κράτος.[52] As the law excluded some individuals from the δῆμος *in potentia* (and, *a fortiori*, from the δῆμος *in actu*), time and space determined the composition of the δῆμος *in actu* at any given ἐκκλησία.[53] In other words, the composition of the assembly varied from meeting to meeting, even if the δῆμος as the singular political agent remained always the same. As for the δῆμος exercising judicial powers (once the transition from the single ἡλιαία to a multiplicity of δικαστήρια had taken place), citizens who wanted to serve in the courts first had to enrol. Six thousand people over the age of 30 were yearly chosen by lot from volunteers. Following this, those who were selected had to swear the judicial oath and, finally, receive a πινάκιον, an official identity card. By 409 BC, the sworn judges were allotted to a different judicial panel each court day: anyone who wished to participate had to be present outside the courts at dawn, bringing his πινάκιον, and he was selected by lot before the further process of assigning cases. Courts including at least 501 citizens heard public cases, while private cases were tried before smaller panels.[54] If, on the one hand, time and space were the main obstacles which impacted the make-up of the assembly at any given time, then, on the other hand, age and sortition (as well as personal choices concerning participation) were factors which marked out judges implicated in the 'rule of the δῆμος *in actu.*'

2.3 Δημοκρατία and new technologies: From Athens to tomorrow?

The picture roughly sketched in this chapter so far has tried to show the flavour of the traditional conception of pure democracy as attested to in antiquity.[55] The form of πολιτεία which explicitly began to emerge in Athens at the end of the 6th century BC was a specific, though that is not to say unparalleled, anti-tyrannical mode of political governance, grounded mainly in the direct will of the majority[56] within the frame of a community of free and equal individuals. Perikles's words in the Funeral Speech reported by Thucydides make this explicit.[57] One of the most astonishing traits of the Athenian democracy is undoubtedly the extraordinary level of participation by the ca. 60,000 adult male citizens in politics. In Athens, ordinary citizens were not only lawgivers and judges who directly exercised the popular κράτος but also acted as counsellors[58] and magistrates[59] invested with a side power called ἀρχή. It is undeniable that for the Athenians, politics was not merely a positive value: It was the very substance of any life worth living, that is to say – as with Aristotle – βίος πολιτικός, both as life in the πόλις and as a πολίτης.[60] According to the Athenian political ideal, participation in the decision-making process was as consistent with human nature as dressing oneself or building houses. Thus politics was an end within itself and not just a means to obtain benefits. Politics was what distinguished human beings from animals. Accordingly, Athenians firmly believed that any πολίτης ought to disregard his self-interest to prevent conflict with political interests and that direct participation in the running of political institutions complied with the idea of a proper βίος πολιτικός. Delegating politics to professional representatives meant violating such an ideal.

In Athens, true democracy was lived by all, not theorised by the few.[61] Such a 'political' and 'democratic' way of life is radically different in comparison to our own. Popular assemblies, where the δῆμος made decisions, have been replaced by parliaments, where representatives decide on behalf of the people without a direct mandate. Sortition has been replaced by election; boards of volunteer magistrates and public prosecutors have been replaced by professional civil servants; annual rotation among all citizens has been forgotten under the weight of a hierarchical bureaucracy of administrators, many of whom serve for decades. Moreover, Athens, by far the largest πόλις in ancient Attika in terms of the size of its adult male citizen body, is miniscule by our standards.[62]

At first, the Athenian scenario may seem an anachronistic model for comprehending the complexities of our times. So considerable is this divide that it prohibits any straightforward application of ancient institutions to our present circumstances. Yet with advancements in digital technology, and in particular the real-time interaction through online communication, it is theoretically possible to replicate the material conditions of an ancient Athenian primary decision-making process.[63] Therefore, if electronic voting can replicate the decision process as determined by a show of hands or by casting the pebble-ballot, those who champion representative democracy can no longer oppose the supporters of direct democracy by arguing that it is a utopian form of government.

Admittedly, the structural uniqueness of the Internet should generally be emphasised as an important opportunity to democratise society to a previously unparalleled degree, bypassing constraints on democracy imposed by the non-digital world and directly expressing the voice of the people. So during the last two generations, institutional and ideological aspects of the Athenian democracy have been taken into consideration as a means to overcome the crisis of our representative democracies. The model of Athenian democracy has, therefore, been seen by an increasing number of scholars, not merely in terms of historic curiosity but also as a real source of inspiration for new forms of popular participation.[64] Accordingly, in considering ancient Athens as a highly relevant paradigm, numerous scholars share the view that the methods used in current democracy are not entirely divorced from the Athenian system; rather, the legal and political system which, in essence, was developed and carried out by the Athenians has simply adapted to new technology. Obviously, no one would dare deny the major differences between ancient and modern democracy, not only in the form of debate at the meetings but also in the way the vote is taken. Nevertheless, some of the basic aspects of democracy are recognisable within both systems so that, direct democracy being technically possible, e-democracy's implementation can undoubtedly be deemed a way to recover the theoretical ancient dispute about the merits of people power and once more make this active. Indeed, rather than focussing on face-to-face assemblies,[65] those who mean to actualise ancient democracy focus on 'selection by lot.' Nowadays, such a figure turns out to be quite marginal if compared to that rooted in the Athenian system.[66] Indeed, 'lot' – obviously removed from its religious connotations – has often been suggested as the optimal way to constitute a small δῆμος that, embodying a cross-section of the entire citizenry (either as an advisory poll panel in combination with a full-scale referendum or as an authentic decision-making body), can gain access to the necessary information and devote enough time and energy to rationally vote after debate and deliberation carried out by tele- or e-communication.[67]

The first to suggest that direct democracy could be given a second life using new technology was Buckminster Fuller.[68] In the 1940s, this architect proposed to conduct referenda electronically, particularly when significant issues were at stake. This would allow for continuous correction of the course without political scapegoating. One of the early intellectual attempts at outlining how technology and participation might be integrated is Wolff's *In Defense of Anarchism*. In a section on instant, direct democracy, he proposes a system of "in-the-home voting machines" that can "transmit...votes...to a computer in Washington."[69]

Burnheim[70] dreamt of a decontaminated democracy fitting our current systems and new technology, a 'demarchy' promoting the correspondence between the character of the representative and the represented; a system where the oligarchical aspect of elections is abandoned and where choice by lot represents the driving force of the state. In this model, government would be divided into small, independent groups of volunteers (selected by lot), and each group – so small that the members could carry on a debate by telecommunication and be sufficiently informed about the political issues at hand

– would be responsible for a different function. All in all, parliaments would be transformed into preparatory and problem-formulating institutions; proposals would be voted on by popular panels and selected by lot from among the entire body of citizens. Sortition, rotation, payment, and the distinction between active and passive participation as aspects drawn from classical Athens would shape the return to a pure democracy.

Inspired by the Athenian example and persuaded that modern technology can revive ancient direct democracy, Schmidt[71] has constructed an elaborate model of modern direct democracy which combines the aforementioned visions of Burnheim and Wolff. According to Schmidt, "Letting four million vote on everything would, even with today's technology, be rather difficult and costly." The solution would be as follows: all Danes would participate in the political decisions by taking it in turns. Considering that Danes are, on average, politically active for 57 years, 4,000,000 divided by 57 gives around 70,000. So, every year in January, 70,000 Danes would be chosen by lot, and for one year they would vote, using a touch-tone phone, for all issues to be considered and debated in Parliament. The following year, another 70,000 electors would be chosen by lot, and so on. Thus for one year in his or her life, every adult Danish citizen would be directly involved in the political decision-making process. Certain important questions would still have to be decided by referendum, yet every political decision would regularly presuppose agreement between the Parliament (Folketing) and MiniDenmark – that is to say, the "electronic second chamber" of 70,000 Danes. If these two bodies disagreed with each other, the matter would be decided by a referendum involving the entire electorate. Therefore, the more times the MiniDenmark voted the same as the Folketing, the fewer referenda there would be.

2.4 Some conclusions

Leaving aside the aforementioned experiments and theories, up to now, e-democracy and e-government, far from capitalising on the potential of the Internet, have, on the contrary, restricted their own role by giving support to current representative democracies. Institutions have thus promoted new technology to foster more transparent forms of government by means of open data to increase political accountability, to simplify petitions and contestations, to make the representatives more approachable, and to attempt to re-involve reluctant citizens.[72]

Empirically, institutional e-government and e-democracy have focussed on setting up democratic platforms and studying the use of the Internet outside of such platforms. For instance, during the 2000s, Italy was far from being a leader in the application of public participation practices, and the Internet was conceived of as a tool merely directed to reduce public costs and increase efficiency. At the national level, the transition to open government policies at the central level only began in 2012 through the publication of the Italian Digital Agenda.[73] Since 2014, participation has primarily taken place through consultations, sometimes even connected with face-to-face discussions, concerning some areas of public law, such as school reform or constitutional and public administration reforms.[74] At the local level, Tuscany was the first region to enact statutes on direct popular participation and to inaugurate open government platforms that combined open data, deliberative forums, and public consultations.[75]

In other words, the institutional platforms basically embrace e-voting, e-petitions, and portals which allow citizens to email their representatives.[76] By supplementing, or replacing, bureaucracy, these advances do not challenge the core problems of current representative democracy, even if they help to reduce the expenses of existing processes or to make these processes more efficient. These core problems include failing to transform government, to reform its political processes, and to foster a mass renewal in popular participation. As far as the aforementioned projects are concerned, they analyse participation occurring on the Internet and study social media as a means to facilitate the organisation of mass movements and even revolutions. Furthermore, this approach to e-democracy fundamentally fails to question the current democratic assets or to promote radical changes to the substance of democracy through technology. In short, the digital world, with all its promising declinations, has often been viewed with myopic pre-digital eyes. No doubt, applying the infrastructure of the Internet to existing political structures may bring quantitative and important results, but it does not directly support the exploration of alternative democratic features. If new technology gives people a voice, only within the capacity to make the electoral system faster and more efficient, I firmly believe the crisis shall continue. On the contrary, past and present systems could work together towards an extreme view of e-democracy. The Athenian paradigm combined with our e-technology knowledge and tools could open the path for facing the crisis that affects our representative democracy, thus founding a new e-δημοκρατία. Naturally, new technology can benefit the public from a formal perspective, but without further fundamental changes, it shall not affect the root of the problem.

Direct democracy, even if implemented through digital instruments, requires a comprehensive and deeply political education among all of its participants. Reducing direct democracy to referenda or to e-voting misses the point, while roughly imitating ancient models fails to grasp Athens's democratic spirit. For instance, Brexit proved a decisive moment in the sad history of our recent democracy. A drastic and vital decision was taken through a 'one-way' referendum based on a simple majority of voters who felt their problems had been ignored by the institutions. On the surface, the fate of the country was democratically determined by the voice of the people; on the surface, the ballot box democratically represented the popular will. Is this the crude and dangerous reality connected to direct democracy? Indeed, the British vote to break away from the EU does not really align with the Athenian model. Athens was aware that democracy gave support to rational and advantageous decisions only if groups and individuals were well informed. Accordingly, the πόλις felt the necessity to promote a broad and totalising political education based upon direct engagement of its citizens with political realities: an Athenian would scorn and deride the idea of committing an irrevocable decision to citizens accustomed to exercising their vote every few years and, above all, only to elect their representatives and delegate this responsibility. In 2016, the Brexit referendum – an Athenian would say – was not a testament of direct democracy. It was a case of political suicide. In Athens, politics was an extremely serious affair, a daily commitment, a constant way of life shared by a significant percentage of the Athenian population. Involvement in the financial, military, and political administration of the city started within the demes, where the holders of locally powerful posts were not, for the most part, men of high socio-economic status. Centrally, aside from the election of a few high magistrates (in particular the board of ten generals), each year, 500 members of the council, 6,000 potential popular judges for the courts, and more than 600 officials were chosen by lot among the eligible male citizens. Such a system was grounded in sortition, together with rules of rotation: a citizen was permitted to serve as a magistrate only once in his lifetime and twice as a councillor, though not in consecutive years. This not only allowed about one-third of the Athenians to have the practical experience of running their democracy but also stimulated a high level of political and bureaucratic awareness. In this context of mass participation, it is not unreasonable that the Athenians should have convened 40 legislative assemblies a year and that the final decision was left to the ordinary citizens. Highly active citizens, on the other hand, in collaboration with the council, were responsible for the initiative and preparation of bills.

Athenian direct democracy was a system based on political participation and on practical experience. These two features changed the mass into a δῆμος. As we have already seen, in democracy, without a δῆμος, there is no κράτος to exercise. Handing the people a referendum every once in a while (or even an e-ballot more frequently) does not give power to the masses. Democracy does not consist of counting the votes. Democracy requires the people as a political body, not as a disaggregated mass, and implies the enactment of the voice of a reasonable sovereign, not of human beings bewildered in the dark and at the mercy of slogans, prejudices, and mysterious forces.

Moreover, an essential tenet rooted in the Athenian democratic ideology holds that the δῆμος is always right: any fault lies not with the voters but with the speakers who misled them. Within this ideological frame, in the 4th century BC, the final ratification of the laws by panels of lawgivers specifically appointed for this purpose by the popular assembly, as well as the judicial review of 'illegal decrees' and of 'laws unsuitably proposed,' were not perceived as restrictions to popular sovereignty. These measures both formalised the popular power to introduce new laws and change existing ones and as such introduced a downstream and upstream protection in favour of the δῆμος and against lying politicians. This meant that a wrong decision, either made directly by the people (through a decree) or previously authorised by the people (and included in a law approved by sworn judges), could be reversed by a popular court on the assumption that the δῆμος had not erred but rather had been deceived by someone who ought to be punished. The people functioned as a sovereign and, as such, had to be considered responsible but not liable. In other words, in Athens, if things go badly because of a bad decision by the sovereign, the sovereign itself can be voiced again. Today, by invoking 'checks and balances' – that is, a principle according to which separate governmental branches are empowered to prevent actions by other branches and are induced to share power – one could see any judiciary's interference as a move to limit what the people or, better, its representatives can do. In Athens, the δῆμος is one, just as the κράτος is one, and neither can be restricted.

Against this background, my hope is that new technologies will not contribute to the enhancement and extension of the crisis affecting the present form of democratic government. On the contrary, I hope that they might work as a suitable instrument to challenge and solve the problems faced by a sick system that – despite its name – shares little or nothing in common with the real δημοκρατία. A sick system that deserves and needs a soft euthanasia to be restarted rather than useless palliative care. The words 'election' and 'democracy' are currently considered synonymous. Yet when the supporters of the American and French revolutions proposed representation as a means to implement 'the will of the people,' there were no parties, no statutes concerning universal franchise, no mass media, and no Internet. Moreover, Athens has taught us that democracy is more than voting and something different from representation. Merge the radical ideas flourished in the past with the digital culture embedded in the present, and the crisis shall be wiped out under the banner of a new e-δημοκρατία.[77]

Notes

1 Cf. Hansen 1989a: 5. See Olechowski 2009: 113.
2 Larsen 1973: esp. 46; Finley 1985: 12; Sinclair 1988: 15; Harrison 1993: 2 f.; Roberts 1994: 14; Rhodes 2003: 18 f.; Dunn 2005: 34; Cartledge 2009: 6; 62; 74; Raaflaub 2007a: esp. 106.
3 Athenian democracy was abolished by the Macedonians in 322 BC and then re-established for shorter and longer periods throughout the 3rd and 2nd centuries. Yet after the Roman conquest in 146 BC, the Greek constitutions became increasingly oligarchical and during the later Hellenistic period democracy vanished from the political scene. During the Enlightenment, the renewed idea of democracy was totally rejected by Madison, Hamilton, Burke, Rousseau, Robespierre, and Bentham, and such negative ideas prevailed in the US (until the new Jacksonian democracy in the 1820s) and in Europe, with the notable exception of Germany (until the revolutions of 1848). Cf. Graeber 2013: ch. 3: "This, then, is what the nightmare vision of Athenian democracy seemed to mean for such men: that if the town hall assemblies and mass meetings of farmers, mechanics, and tradesmen that had formed in the years leading up to the Revolution became institutionalised, these – 'abolition of debts...equal division of property' – were the sorts of demands they would likely make. Even more, they feared the spectre of orgy, tumult, and indiscipline, where the sort of grave republicans who led Rome to glory and whom the Founders saw as their model would be cast aside for the vulgar passions of the masses."
4 Cf. Hansen 2005: 13 ff., on the political use of Perikles and Demosthenes as symbols of democracy in UK and in France during the first half of the 20th century. On the reception of the idea of Athenian democracy, see Piovan - Giorgini (eds.) 2021: *passim*.

5 Draft treaty establishing a constitution for Europe (10.6.2003): "Preamble: Our constitution…is called a democracy because power is in the hands not of a minority but of the greatest number." During the revision of the draft, in June 2004, the Intergovernmental Conference of Brussels dropped the quote from the final version (CIG 87/04).

6 Cf. Miller 2018: 245.

7 Cf. Donlan 1970; Ober 2008a; Cartledge 2009: 74; Hansen 2010; Osborne 2010: 42.

8 Arist. *Pol.* 1278b, 1290a30–b20; cf. [Xen.] *Ath. Pol.* 2.20; Plat. *Resp.* 565e.

9 Cf. [Xen.] *Ath. Pol.* 1.4, 1.18. Athenagoras was reported by Thucydides to have boasted at a meeting of the Syracusan assembly that the δῆμος was the best at listening and judging and that the noun δῆμος stood for the whole (ξύμπαν), while oligarchy for only a part (Thuc. 6.39). Demosthenes claimed that the allies had crowned the δῆμος for courage and righteousness (Dem. 24.180) and that in Sparta, there were honours that ἅπας ὁ δῆμος would not like to introduce in Athens (Dem. 20.106); Dinarchus himself states that "you and the δῆμος as a whole risk losing the foundations of the πόλις, the ancestral temples, and your wives and children" (Din. 1.99). Cf., moreover, *IG* II² 26.8–9; *IG* I³ 110.6–9; *IG* II² 97.6–8; 116.27–28. The 4th century orators qualify the Athenian regime in terms of δημοκρατία, never contrasting it with the kingship of the law: cf. e.g. Dem. 59.88; Aeschin. 1.4–6, 3.6–7; Lyc. 1.3.

10 Ober 2008a: 3 ff.

11 [Arist.] *Ath. Pol.* 41.

12 Aristoph. *Eq.* 42–43: 751.

13 Thuc. 2.37.1–2; Arist. *Pol.* 1310a28–33 (cf. 1291b33; 1318a9); Isoc. 7.20; Plat. *Resp.* 563b. Cf., on the triangle 'democracy, freedom, equality,' Holden 1974: 5; Holden 1988: 5. On equality and liberties as prerequisites for the practice of direct democracy, see Raaflaub 2008. Cf., in general terms, Forrest 1966: 44, who deems democracy as a system that embodies "the idea that all members of a political society are free and equal, that everyone had the right to an equal say in determining the structure and the activities of his society"; see, similarly, Farrar 1988: 11; 104.

14 Solon fr. 36.1–2 (West): ἐγὼ δὲ τῶν μὲν οὕνεκα ξυνήγαγον / δῆμον, τί τούτων πρὶν τυχεῖν ἐπαυσάμην.

15 Cf. Sol. fr. 36.18–20 (West): θεσμοὺς δ' ὁμοίως τῷ κακῷ τε κἀγαθῷ, / εὐθεῖαν εἰς ἕκαστον ἁρμόσας δίκην, / ἔγραψα. In my opinion, it is reasonable to interpret these lines as an implicit mention to the written laws which introduced the figure of ὁ βουλόμενος (i.e. "popular prosecution by anyone who wishes" [Arist.] *Ath. Pol.* 9.1 [ἔπειτα τὸ ἐξεῖναι τῷ βουλομένῳ τιμωρεῖν ὑπὲρ τῶν ἀδικουμένων]) and the legal procedure of ἔφεσις to the ἡλιαία (i.e. 'appeal' to the popular court: [Arist.] *Ath. Pol.* 9.1 [τρίτον δὲ <ᾧ καὶ> μάλιστά φασιν ἰσχυκέναι τὸ πλῆθος, ἡ εἰς τὸ δικαστήριον ἔφεσις· κύριος γὰρ ὢν ὁ δῆμος τῆς ψήφου, κύριος γίγνεται τῆς πολιτείας]). In other words, Solon made 'peers of unequals' since anyone belonging to the Athenian people, regardless of his timocratical class, was entitled to raise a popular action and to vote in the popular court. The governing principle was the formal political equality of all citizens.

Athenians, rich and poor alike, held an equal share in exercising the κράτος: cf. Pelloso 2014–2015: esp. 31 ff. In the same context and in view of the same targets, Solon made it illegal to own Athenians as slaves, implying that all Athenians were equal: cf. Ober 2008b.

16 Sartori 1968: esp. 112.

17 Solon fr. 36.1–2 (West).

18 Solon is said to have introduced 'ἔφεσις to the popular court,' establishing the Athenian people as a 'body' endowed with the power of giving final judgements and superseding magisterial decisions: cf. Pelloso 2016a; Pelloso 2017a. Indeed, a word-for-word translation of [Arist.] *Ath. Pol.* 9.1 leads the interpreter to assume that the 6th century BC lawgiver just 'renewed' and 'strengthened' an existing body (the δῆμος) by giving it judicial powers and opening it up to everyone: cf. Plut. *Sol.* 18.2; [Arist.] *Ath. Pol.* 7.3.

19 Wolin 1994; Ober 2007.

20 Before Solon's reforms were enacted, magistrates were both κύριοι (i.e. qualified to pass decisions that could not be amended or quashed) and αὐτοτελεῖς (i.e. qualified to start *ex officio* legal procedures): cf. [Arist.] *Ath. Pol.* 3.5. Thanks to Solon, people and magistrates started contributing to the governing of the city as opposing powers, each endowed with their own prerogatives, even if the former's supremacy was, in the 4th century BC, an indisputable feature of the Athenian regime. In the *Politics*, likewise, Aristotle considered Athenian courts to be one of the most demotic traits of Solon's system and identified them as the way the δῆμος had achieved the highest status possible within the entire community, even increasing the majority's power after the reforms which took place in 403–402 BC (Arist. *Pol.* 1273b36–1274a23; cf. [Arist.]. *Ath. Pol.* 9.1, 10.1, 25.2, 27.4, 29.4, 35, 41.2, 45.1–45.3, 49.3, 63–68, 53.1, 55.3–55.4).

21 For the Solonian democracy as a historical myth and for the Kleisthenic origins of the Athenian δημοκρατία as the Athenians' description of their own constitution (cf. Hdt. 6.131), see Hansen 1989c: esp. 77–82, and Hansen 1994 (but cf. Arist. *Pol.* 1273b35–74a5, cf. [Arist.] *Ath. Pol.* 9.1, 42.1); see, moreover, Hansen 2005: 11 ff. on the praise, in the 18th century, of the moderate mixed constitution introduced by Solon. Conversely, according to Raaflaub, it seems a more tenable guess that Athens became a democracy only after the reforms introduced by Ephialtes in 462–461 (Raaflaub 2007a), even if he admits that there is no need to imitate the Greeks in seeking the 'first inventor' (πρῶτος εὑρετής) of democracy (Raaflaub 2007b: 16).

22 Cf. Pelloso 2017: 526, n. 23.

23 [Arist.] *Ath. Pol.* 8.4.

24 Cf. Andoc. 1.96–98; Hyp. 4.7–8; Lyc. 1.125–26; *SEG* 12.87; Aristoph. *Eccl.* 453; Thuc. 1.107, 5.76, 8.64–5; Aeschin. 1.173, 191; Arist. *Pol.* 1304a27, 1304b30–34, 1307b24; *IG* II³ 1.320. In terms of [Arist.] *Ath. Pol.* 8.4, Ostwald persuasively argues that such a law was really passed under Solon, but at the same time, he maintains that "since later legislation differentiated κατάλυσις τοῦ δήμου at least verbally from attempts at establishing tyranny, and since the law under discussion was not invoked against the Peisistratids after their overthrow, it makes more sense to see

in Aristotle's description a reflection of a broader measure, designed to protect the public institutions of Athens against any kind of subversion, that is against any crime against the state"; moreover, the scholar assumes that this particular statement is anachronistic only "if we understand by εἰσαγγελία the complex procedure that in the fifth and fourth centuries involved the Council and the Assembly or the jury colts": Ostwald 1986: 8; Almeida 2003: 65 f.

25 These reflections raise the following question: Does a genuine European people exist? No doubt, the global financial crisis in 2008 has disclosed all the deficiencies of Europe's monetary union, prompting a savage and acrimonious debate over fiscal union. Sharing a common currency without sharing a real budget has proven to be unstable and dangerous; the Hamiltonian idea that a common debt represents a blessing and a powerful cement has never taken hold in the EU (where, on the contrary, providing emergency loans and cheap debts has always been the preferred route) or, at least, until recently. Indeed, while the first European summits of the COVID-19 crisis held during the spring of 2020 consistently revealed a deep lack of cohesion and solidarity, things seem to have changed with the beginning of summer. The EU leaders, including the reluctant "Frugals" (who have obtained rebates for their contributions to the EU budget, as well as the power to veto disbursements if displeased with the reforms undertaken by the shaky Mediterranean economies), have agreed upon a course which seemed impossible over the last decade: for the first time, a breakthrough post-pandemic EU recovery deal that authorises the European Commission to issue bonds and 750 billion Euros will be borrowed jointly by member states in proportion to their capacity so as to be spent in proportion to their needs. Thus, finally, not only common debt and common expenditure but also the possibility of common taxation have resulted in a significant step towards unity in the EU.

26 Cf. Hansen 1999: 178 ff.; 225 f.; 247.

27 Raaflaub 2007b: 16.

28 Cf. *ML* 5.11, 14.1; *RO* 31.7, 41.3–4; Aeschin. 2.17; Dem. 18.248, 24.9. Cf. Larsen 1973: 46: "The greatest victory for the common people in the development of democracy at Athens was that the name for their group became the word used to designate the sovereign people in the records of votes in the assembly." According to Ober 1996: 107, the literary figure of synecdoche would explain the relationship between assembly and δῆμος since the former (a part of the whole citizen body) stands for, and refers to, the latter (the whole citizen body); conversely, Cammack 2019: 58 attempts to demonstrate that the main meaning of δῆμος was 'mass' with the exclusion of the elite: "It was not that the assembly (part) came to be called δῆμος (whole) because the entire community (πόλις) was imagined to meet on the Pnyx, but that the δῆμος (part) came to be called πόλις (whole) because acted on behalf of, or in other words ruled, the πόλις."

29 Hansen 2010: 507.

30 Hdt. 6.131.1, 5.69.2; [Arist.] *Ath. Pol.* 21.2–4; Arist. *Pol.* 1319b19–27; see also Schol. anonim. 10, 13 (Diehl II, 184); [Arist.] *Ath. Pol.* 13.2.

31 Hdt. 6.131; cf. [Arist.] *Ath. Pol.* 20.1 and Hdt. 5.66.2.

32 Rooted in the field of constitutional law, such a shift was fundamental, as it

transformed an assembly that was only allowed to claim the θεσμοί (i.e. rules imposed by individual legislators like Drako and Solon) into an assembly entitled to approve or reject proposals of νόμοι by exercising its own new κράτος. Even though direct evidence is flimsy, this view would gain further support, according to Ostwald, if one reads it in light of the semantic passage that occurred at the end of the 6th century – i.e. almost at the same time of Kleisthenes's reforms – and fixed the word νόμος "as an expression of what the people as a whole regarded as a valid and binding norm." Kleisthenes's constitution definitely provided "the background for the change from θεσμός to νόμος": cf. Ostwald 1969: 9; 20; 54 ff.; cf., moreover, Ehrenberg 1921: 103 ff.; Dihle 1995; Gschnitzer 1997. Kleisthenes, in other words, created a precedent: as if "it seems a reasonable guess that it was in the Assembly" that the Athenian leader "allied himself to the δῆμος, by proposing (and perhaps actually passing) constitutional reforms" (Ober 1996: 38). Ever since that concession was granted, the popular κράτος was mainly conceived of as a manifestation of a legislative power.

33 A single individual being commonly the authority which made decisions for the δῆμος (i.e. those who are ruled), in democracies, such a role was played by the δῆμος as the popular assembly. In Aeschylus's *Suppliants* (ca. 463 BC) the phrase δήμου κρατοῦσα χείρ ("the ruling hand of the δῆμος") suggests the vote was taken by means of the show of hands in assembly (l. 604, cf. 699); in Euripides's *Suppliants* (ca. 423 BC), Theseus claims that he has established the δῆμος as a monarch by freeing the citizens (cf., for liberty as political participation by ruling in turn, Thuc. 2.37.1–2, 40.2; Isoc. 20.20) and giving them equal votes (ll. 352–353) so that "the δῆμος rules as a sovereign (ἀνάσσει)" (l. 406); Aeschines (3.233) argues that through law and voting the ordinary citizen rules as a king (βασιλεύει); Aristotle describes δημοκρατία as a radical system where the δῆμος (i.e. the mob), and not the νόμος, plays the role of the monarch, to such an extent that decrees were given even higher authority than laws (Arist. *Pol.* 1298b13–15, 1292a12). These remarks are a clear political exaggeration, forgetting the distinction, introduced by law, existing between a decree and a statute, as well as the hierarchical prevalence of the latter on the former (cf. Dem. 24.18, 59). Since only nine *stelai* preserve epigraphically laws passed in the 4th century, while we have around 500 decrees (cf. Hansen 1978; Canevaro 2011: esp. 57 n. 7), implied by Aristotle is the following simple datum: the Athenians, rather than infringing on the aforementioned distinction and implementing a general limitation of popular sovereignty much to the benefit of popular courts (cf. Kahrstedt 1938; Hansen 1974: 15 ff.; Hansen 1990: 239 ff.; Hansen 1999: 150 f.; 156 f.; 351 f.; *contra*, see Atkinson 1939), continued to give the assembly most political business – that is, alongside day-to-day administration, the decretal extraordinary regulation, the number of which was clearly more than that of the laws. What is more, as Cartledge 2016: 223 rightly observes, "There was no modern notion of the separation of powers in the Classical Athenian democratic πόλις, and no Supreme Court." This means that maintaining a limitation on the sovereignty of the people in the 4th century BC amounts to nonsense.

34 From another perspective, see Bodin 1962: 705: "If we shall rip up all the popular states that ever were, we shall find that…they have been governed

in show by the people; but in effect by some of the citizens, or by the wisest among them, who held the place of a prince and monarch."
35 Cf. the celebrated funeral speech given by Perikles where democracy is bound, among other principles, to the law (Thuc. 2.37) and, moreover, the words Euripides attributes to Theseus, depicted as an anachronistic supporter of the democratic values (Eur. *Suppl.* 404–407, 433–437). See Lys. 2.17–19; Aeschin. 1.1–7, 23, 36–37, 179, 3.6–7, 23; Dem. 7.7, 21.30, 34, 76, 177, 222–225, 22.57, 23.1, 97, 190, 24.2, 36–37, 215–216, 26.6, 28.278, 283–284, 290–293, 306–309; Din. 3.16; Hyp. *Epitaph.* 6.25 (Colin); Lyc. 1.3–6, 138; Lys. 26.15, 31.2. The so-called rule of law – or rather the kingship of νόμος – far from being a mere slogan, played a fundamental role on the institutional, ideological, and practical levels within the democratic context of 5th- and 4th-century Athens: see, paradigmatically, Harris 2013, Pelloso 2017–2018, and Gagarin 2020.
36 For the first clause, see Aeschin. 3.6; Dem. 20.118. See, for further references, Aeschin. 3.31, 198; Andoc. 1.2, 4.9; Ant. 5.85; Dem. 8.2, 18.121, 21.42, 211, 22.7, 20, 43, 23.2, 101, 24.188, 34.45, 52, 36.26, 39.41, 43.34, 46.27, 52.33, 58.25, 36, 56, 59.115; Din. 1.17, 84; Hyp. 2.5, 5.1, 39; Isae. 6.65, 11.6; Isoc. 15.173, 19.15, 44, 46; Lyc. 1.143; Lys. 9.19, 10.32, 14.22, 22.7. This clause, requiring the judges to decide according to the laws, was the most frequently cited, which means that, in the context of a trial, it was the most important: cf. Pelloso 2017.
37 Judicial bodies, from the 6th century ἡλιαία to the late 5th century and 4th century δικαστήρια, were direct manifestations of the δῆμος and could even be perceived of as the Athenian people within a judicial capacity (either gathered as a whole or divided into several panels): cf. Hignett 1952: 233; Gomme 1962: 188; Forrest 1966: 19; 166; Rhodes 1972: 168; Finley 1985: 116 ff.; Ostwald 1986: 9 ff.; 28 ff.; Ober 1989: 96 f.; Cammack 2017 (expected but unpublished); Carugati - Weingast 2018: esp. 165 f.; 173 and n. 29. On the shift from the ἡλιαία to the δικαστήρια (and, at the same time, on the transfer of the magisterial personal jurisdiction to the popular courts, for which in the 4th century the archons would lead the preliminary examination's hearing and preside over the trial phase), see Ostwald 1986: 69 ff.; 74 ff.
38 Dem. 21.30, 34, 76, 177, 22.57, 24.36, 25.6; Din. 3.16; Aeschin. 1.7, 3.7. Moreover, among the Athenians, there was a firm belief that ancestors established the popular courts, not for the Athenians to dispute their personal grievances but to determine whether someone had carried out misconduct against the πόλις and committed wrongs for which the laws provided penalties (Dem. 18.123, 23.1; Aeschin. 1.1–2; Lys. 31.2, 26.15). At the same time, the duty of the just citizen, in the quality of public prosecutor, was to prevent the bringing to trial of those who had caused no public harm for the sake of private quarrels only. A prosecutor had to accuse those who had violated the law as personal enemies and to view crimes affecting the community as causes of private and public enmity (Lyc. 1.6).
39 Lys. 15.9; cf. Dem. 23.96–23.97, 57.63.
40 Andoc. 1.17, 22; Wolff 1969; Ostwald 1986: 125 ff.; 135 f.; Hansen 1989b: 271 ff.; Hansen 1999: 205 ff.; Pasquino 2005; Pasquino 2010; Lanni 2010.

41 In the 4th century BC, after the introduction of the indictment against inexpedient laws, the γραφὴ παρανόμων started being used only against decrees and continued to be considered a pivotal instrument for protecting democracy: no decree could override a law, and if any was found to be in conflict, it could be abolished by means of a legal procedure started by anyone who wished to: Plat. *Def.* 415b; Dem. 24.18, 59, 58.34; cf. Hansen 1983: 161 ff.; 179 ff.; cf. Hansen 1978: 315 ff.

42 To be more precise, the indictment against illegal proposals was not perceived, in the first place, as a sort of self-restraint: The democratic ideology was such as to imply that, if the people committed a mistake, this only depended upon the speakers who had misled most of the voters ([Xen.] *Ath. Pol.* 2.17; Thuc. 2.59, 8.1; Xen. *Hell.* 1.7.35; Dem. 20.3–4, 23.97; [Arist.] *Ath. Pol.* 28.3). Accordingly, the γραφὴ παρανόμων was primarily directed to annul the effects of an illegal – that is, superseding an established law – proposal and, therefore, to protect the democratic *status quo* against any possible subversion of the order by the members of the elite (cf. Farrar 2007, and Sundahl 2003: esp. 137). It is not by chance that during the so-called 411 "coup de Etat," one of the highest priorities of the oligarchs was the abolition of the procedure of impeachment for speakers, as well as of the γραφὴ παρανόμων; likewise, such a measure was in the agenda both of the Thirty, in 404 BC, and of Antipater, in 322 BC. Indeed, the oligarchs, to go back to the ancestral statutes enacted in the 7th and 6th centuries BC, had to dismiss as illegal all the subsequent democratic enactments (i.e., above all, the laws of Ephialtes and Archestratus): yet these reforms entailed so profound a legal change that in order to be carried out completely, it was necessary to abolish the procedure of γραφὴ παρανόμων (cf. [Arist.] *Ath. Pol.* 29.4; Thuc. 8.67.2; Aeschin. 3.191).

43 For instance, in 406 BC, after the successful battle of the Arginusai, the Athenians punished their generals for failing to rescue numerous men who were shipwrecked (Xen. *Hell.* 1.6–7). The council authorised the proposal that the generals should be tried as a board before the people. Someone intervened to claim that such a legal procedure was against the law since criminals had to be prosecuted and brought to court as individuals, yet the objection was rejected as unsustainable (Xen. *Hell.* 1.7.12). In the end, the generals were condemned and executed: Too late, the people realised its own misbehaviour and regretted as παράνομν its own conduct (Xen. *Hell.* 1.7.35).

44 Cf. Sealey 1987: 146 (thinking that the Athenians pursued the rule of law, not democracy), Ostwald 1986: 524 (adhering to the idea that the creation of rules of legal change meant in Athens a limitation of popular sovereignty and that the turn of the 4th century attests to a shift from a form of radical democracy to the sovereignty of the law), and Hansen 1999: 150 ff. (sharing the view that the Athenians pursued popular sovereignty in the 5th century, the rule of law in the 4th century, or better that from the beginning of the 4th century everything decided by the Athenian assembly could be overturned by a court, but what a court decided could not be overturned by the assembly, this meaning a shift from the supremacy of the assembly to the supremacy of the courts). These views have rightly been challenged: cf. Blanshard 2004, who

stresses that no source states that the Athenians regarded the judiciary as a restraint on the assembly of the people; Harris 2016: 73 ff., makes it clear that Athenian courts, constituted by men of the people (and not by officials), were no less democratic than the assembly so that a shift of tasks from one body to the other neither mattered in terms of restraint nor amounted to the passage from the rule of assembly to the rule of law. Along the same lines of thinking are the following authors: Canevaro 2015: esp. 21 ff., who argues that the new procedure of law-making together with the indictments for illegal decrees and for inexpedient laws did not limit popular sovereignty but recognised and formalised the right to introduce new laws and change existing ones; Cammack 2017 (expected but unpublished), who supports the idea that judicial panels represented the rule of the people even better than the assembly; see also Piovan 2017–2018.

45 Cf. Canevaro 2013a: 80 ff.; 102 ff.; Canevaro 2013b; Canevaro 2019.

46 In order to introduce a new law, the first step was the preliminary vote in the assembly preceded by a prior authorisation of the council at any point in the year; then the proposal had to be published before the monument of the Eponymous Heroes and read out by the secretary in each assembly until the appointment of the νομοθέται; opposing laws had to be repealed before the enactment of the new laws; presumably at the same time of the appointment of the νομοθέται, συνήγοροι were chosen to defend the established laws whose repeal was necessary for enacting the new laws. I have tried to summarise the essence of the reforms concerning legal change on two points: prohibition of tacit repeal (Dem. 24.32-34 and Dem. 20.93–96) and prohibition of pure repeal (Dem. 20.88–89 and Dem. 24.33; cf. Dem. 3.10–11): cf. Pelloso 2016: 38, n. 103 (adhering to many of the ideas supported by Canevaro 2016, even if I argue that Dem. 20.89 neither states that "bringing a public action is…necessary only if one believes that one of the existing laws are not good, and not in order to propose any new law" nor refers "to the rule that when one proposed a new law, one needed first of all to repeal any contradictory laws"; indeed, the orator considers the case where the main focus is not on introducing a new law, as it is in Dem. 24.32–4 and 93, but – quite the opposite – in repealing an existing νόμος deemed as οὐ καλός and, consequently, in filling the nomic gap with a new enactment).

47 Cf. Dem. 24.1, 34.68–71, 108, 138–141.

48 In a similar fashion, see Cammack 2019: 42 ff., even if the author, in her scrupulous diachronic overview, seems to sketch an excessively monistic picture. For instance, how can the people be labelled as an 'active' (i.e. vested with political capacity) and, at the same time, 'partial' (i.e. not including the elite) agent in Hom. *Il.* 18.497 ff. and in Hom. *Od.* 8.555, 13.233? Indeed, on the one side, the trial scene of the shield attests to an interchangeable use of δῆμος and λαοί and depicts the crowd gathered in the ἀγορή as a mass without any judicial power; on the other side, the two Odyssey's *loci* confirm that the members of the elite belonged to a given δῆμος.

49 Cf., generally, [Arist.] *Ath. Pol.* 42.1; see, moreover, Andoc. 1.73, 75; Lys. 10.1.

50 It is a widespread criticism that, grounded in the deep divide between ancient and modern democracies, has led some authors to conceive of Athens as a pointless example: cf. Bryce 1921: 207; Bentham 1960: 68, n. 2; Dahl 1989: 3; Budge 1996: 26; Paladin 1998: 148.

51 Hansen 1999: 90 ff.: in Athens, the number of full citizens may have been as high as 50,000 in the mid-5th century, but that number declined significantly (due to plagues and warfare) to around 30,000. Total population ranged between 250,000 and 400,000 people, including around 100,000 citizen households (Athenian men, women, children), in addition to tens of thousands of metics and 100,000 (or more) slaves.

52 The ἐκκλησία consisted of a meeting formally called out (cf. Hansen 2010: 507; Cammack 2019: 53 ff.) where, after a debate, an issue was decided by a majority vote taken by a show of hands: the ἐκκλησία.

53 Cf. Hansen 1999: 71 f.; 90 ff.; 143 ff.; 306 ff.; 312. In the 4th century BC, every year the Athenians summoned 40 ἐκκλησίαι attended by around 6,000 citizens (about a fifth of the citizen population) that regularly turned up to debate and vote political issues presented to the people after a prior consideration by the council. Initiative and decision were separate activities so that highly active citizens (i.e. the ideal *rhetores*: Thuc. 6.39.1; Aeschin. 3.220), in collaboration with the council, were in charge of initiative and preparation of bills, whereas appropriate silence during the speeches and voting according to the laws were what was expected from the ideal ordinary citizens (Dem. 10.70–4, 18.308, 19.99, 22.30; Aeschin. 3.233; Eur. *Suppl.* 438–441; Hdt. 5.78; [Xen.] *Ath. Pol.* 1.2; Plat. *Gorg.* 461e, and *Prot.* 319b–d, 322d–23a). Obviously, political participation was paid so that it was possible for low-class citizens to exercise their political rights: Perikles enacted the provision of payment for judging, whereas payment for attending the assembly was introduced later ([Arist.] *Ath. Pol.* 27.3–4, 41.3, 62.2; Plat. *Gorg.* 515e; cf. Aristoph. *Eccl.* 289, 309–10; see Markle 1985).

54 Boegehold 1995: 22 ff.

55 Cf. Cartledge 2016.

56 By deepening and taking advantage of some of the ideas in the work of Musti 1995, Canevaro 2018, has recently argued that the institutional set-up of the assembly, together with its *ethos*, was geared towards reaching consensus – that is, unanimous or quasi-unanimous decisions.

57 Thuc. 2.37.1–3: "Our form of government does not enter into rivalry with the institutions of others. We do not copy our neighbours but are an example to them. It is true that we are called a democracy, for the administration is in the hands of the many and not of the few. But while the law secures equal justice to all alike in their private disputes, the claim of excellence is also recognised; and when a citizen is in any way distinguished, he is preferred to the public service, not as a matter of privilege, but as the reward of merit. Neither is poverty a bar, but a man may benefit his country whatever be the obscurity of his condition. [2] There is no exclusiveness in our public life, and in our private intercourse we are not suspicious of one another, nor angry with our neighbour if he does what he likes; we do not put on sour looks at him which, though harmless, are not pleasant. [3] While we are thus unconstrained in our private

intercourse, a spirit of reverence pervades our public acts; we are pre-
vented from doing wrong by respect for the authorities and for the laws,
having an especial regard to those which are ordained for the protection
of the injured as well as to those unwritten laws which bring upon the
transgressor of them the reprobation of the general sentiment" (Trans.
Benjamin Jowett); see Dem. 18.273; [Arist.] *Ath. Pol.* 45.2; besides, cf.
Dem. 3.15.

58 The council of the 500 citizens was a yearly magisterial board in which
most Athenians served at least once (Hansen 1999: 313 f.) and mirrored
the whole community since its members where drawn from the whole of
Attika; it was responsible for the everyday affairs of the city and prepar-
ing the agenda of the assembly.

59 Every year, a massive number of magistrates and public officers were
selected by lot and served a short-term office (usually a year) together
with a ban on iteration to guarantee the highest degree of rotation:
Hansen 1999: 197 ff.; 225 ff.; 235 ff.; 308.

60 Thuc. 2.40.2: "An Athenian citizen does not neglect the state because he
takes care of his own household; and even those of us who are engaged
in business have a very fair idea of politics. We alone regard a man who
takes no interest in public affairs, not as a harmless, but as a useless character; and if few of us are originators, we are all sound judges of a
policy"; Thuc. 6.39.1: "I shall be told that democracy is neither a wise
nor a just thing, and that those who have the money are most likely to
govern well. To which I answer, first of all, that the people is the name of
the whole, the oligarchy of a part; secondly, that the rich are the best
guardians of the public purse, the wise the best counsellors, and the
many, when they have heard a matter discussed, the best judges; [2] and
that each and all of these classes have in a democracy equal privileges"
(Trans. Benjamin Jowett); Arist. *Pol.* 1283b42–1284a2: "πολῖται in the
common sense of that term, are all who share in the civil life of ruling and
being ruled in turn…and under an ideal constitution they must be those
who are able and willing to rule and be ruled with a view to attaining a
way of life according to goodness."

61 Brock 1991.

62 Cf. Cohen 1989: 30; Schaub 2012. Yet see Beard 2016: "Ancient Athens
is far too different from us for that: its citizen body was, for a start, no
larger than the size of some modern university student unions, and was
completely 'woman-free.' But Athens can help us to look harder at ourselves. Handing us a referendum once every twenty years or so, largely
depriving us of accurate information in a fog of slogans and rhetoric, and
allowing us all, on both sides, to vent our various discontents and prejudices in a yes/no vote is not a way to reach a responsible decision. Nor is
it a way to re-empower a disempowered electorate. That, as Athenian
democrats would have seen, needs something much more radical, and it
has to happen not twice in a lifetime but in the day-to-day practice of
political life."

63 Dahl 1989: 340 suggests one model of democracy which incorporates the
following features: "Suppose an advanced democratic country were to
create a *minipopulus* consisting of perhaps a thousand citizens randomly
selected out of the entire δῆμος. Its task would be to deliberate, for a year

perhaps, on an issue and then to announce its choices. The members of a *minipopulus* could 'meet' by telecommunications…The judgment of a *minipopulus* would 'represent' the judgment of the δῆμος. Its verdict would be the verdict of the δῆμος itself." Cf. Grossman 1995: 239 ff.; Qvortrup 2007; Kneuer 2016. For a rather critical approach, see Katz 1997: 96; see, moreover, Barney 2000; Gibson - Römmele - Ward 2004.

64 Cf., for instance, McLean 1989: 158: "Could we reinvent Athenian democracy; more pedantically, some combination of democracy and demarchy that was at least as good as the Athenians'? It would have to be better in one regard: it must be workable in an entire population, and not restricted to free men."

65 Even if the ancient Athenian model as a direct democracy remains unparalleled, face-to-face assemblies can be studied so as to analyse contemporary institutions. Indeed, at the subnational level, there are several examples which resemble Athens 2,500 years ago: for instance, in the Swiss *Landsgemeinde*, in the New England Town Meetings, and in the Israeli *Kibbutzim*, all members are allowed to voice their concerns by means of face-to-face deliberation and, eventually, by a direct vote: cf. Altman 2019: 180 f.

66 As Van Reybrouck 2016a maintains, "The plebiscite is probably the worst way of sampling public opinion and that we would be better off reverting to the classical-era Athenian practice of sortition – decision-making by large randomly-selected juries"; moreover, see Van Reybrouck 2016b. According to Barber 1984: 280; 289, "The lot principle…is a natural extension of the democratic principle to large-scale societies," and "when the representatives to the town meetings are chosen by lot and membership is rotated, over time all will be able to participate"; in his opinion, "electronic balloting…carefully used, can enhance democracy" and "feedback-polls…can be a valuable instrument of civic education." Cf. Carson - Martin 1999; Sintomer 2007.

67 The case of the British Columbia in 2004–2005 is exemplary: The Liberal Party, bypassing the legislation, invested a citizens' assembly (composed of 160 ordinary citizens, one man and one woman selected by lot from each district) on an important constitutional matter in order to formulate a proposal and submit it to a referendum (the final report can be downloaded from: http:// citizensassembly.arts.ubc.ca/resources/final_report. pdf; see, for a similar initiative, Australia's Citizens Parliament: www.citizensparliament.org.au). Following on from this episode, Ferejohn has suggested that a citizens' assembly should be automatically convened anytime an initiative is proposed; this assembly, mirroring the whole electorate, would be expected to take the time necessary to achieve an adequate level of expertise and to draft an informed proposal for the electorate in view of a referendum (Ferejohn 2008: 212). Conversely, Fishkin believes the citizens' panel ("a large enough sample for the responses to be statistically meaningful, but small enough to be practical") would neither decide the issue nor would propose a solution: The poll would merely work as a guideline for the electorate when citizens were called to vote: cf. Fishkin 2006; Farrar - Fishkin - Green - List - Luskin - Levy Paluck 2010. Cf., on the Icelandic constitutional reform process of 2010 (where a constitutional assembly composed of 25

citizens was appointed to write, with the support of legal experts, a new constitutional document based on the outcomes of a national assembly of a random sample of 950 Icelanders), Landemore 2015.
68 Fuller 1980; Toffler 1980; Naisbitt 1982; Becker 1998; Becker - Slaton 2000. Cf. also Arterton 1987.
69 Wolff 1970: 34 f.
70 Burnheim 1985: 115; cf. Burnheim 2016.
71 Schmidt 2001 and Schmidt 1993.
72 "By Electronic Democracy or eDemocracy, we understand the support and enhancement of civil rights and duties in the information and knowledge society. In the centre of attention stand options of participation, which, by the aid of information and communication technology, can be carried out time- and location-independently: Inclusion of the citizens even in early stages of clarification and planning by the public entities, improved information and discussion policy that is suited to the citizens' requirements, barrier-free Web access in electronic votes and elections, formation of communities in different public sectors and for different social concerns, practice of civil rights on all communal levels and improvement of political controlling by use of adequate archiving and documentation systems. By means of eDemocracy and the possibilities of participation that come along with it, the information society is to develop into a knowledge society. The primary target of this is not the creation of new rights and duties for the citizens, but an extended information policy, activation of citizens, community formation, and creation of transparency" (Meier - Terán 2019: 3).
73 The Italian Digital Agenda was established on 1 March 2012 by decree of the minister of economic development in agreement with the minister for public administration and simplification; the minister of territorial cohesion; the minister of education, university, and research; and the minister of economy and finance. It transferred strategies and principles outlined by the Digital Agenda for Europe into the Italian system through a plan of initiatives and measures, as well as through a synergy among public powers at the central and local levels. Moreover, in the framework of the Partnership Deal 2014–2020, the Presidency of the Council of Ministers together with the Ministry for Economic Development, the Agency for Digital Italy, and the Agency for Territorial Cohesion have provided the national plans "Digital Growth" and "Ultra-wide Band National Plan" in view of the achievement of the Digital Agenda's goals. As for the *status quo*, see https://joinup.ec.europa.eu/sites/default/files/inline-files/Digital_Government_Factsheets_Italy_2019_0.pdf.
74 In May 2014, the Italian government began to work on a reform concerning the hiring and governance practices within the public education system. The so-called *Buona Scuola* became law (n. 107/2015) having been at the centre of one of the most extensive public e-consultation experiments held in Italy.
75 On the grounds of two regional laws (n. 69/2007: i.e. the first regional law on public participation in Italy; n. 46/2013: i.e. the act that gave the regional government a legal mandate to "renew democracy and its institutions by integrating them with practices, processes and tools of participatory democracy"), Tuscany – through the Tuscany Regional Participation

Policy, a pioneering instrument for the institutionalisation of public participation and deliberation – has promoted participation as a regular form of government, involving different bodies, agencies, and sectors of the public administration and civil society. Cf. Lewanski 2013; see also https://participedia.net/method/5594;http://www.consiglio.regione.toscana.it/upload/AUTORIT%C3%80%20PARTECIPAZIONE/documenti/legge-2013-00046.pdf.

76 Suffice it to say that the process of drafting the Treaty of Rome of 2004 – i.e. the treaty containing a constitution for Europe – also included the participation of citizens through an online forum (cf. Cerulli Irelli 2006: 60 ff.).

77 "It is fully conceivable that one day through ingenious discoveries, every single person, without leaving his apartment, could continuously express his opinions on political questions through an apparatus and that all these opinions would automatically be registered by a central office, where one would only need to read them off" (Schmitt 2008: 274).

Bibliography

J.A. Almeida, *Justice as an Aspect of the Polis Idea in Solon's Political Poems. A Reading of the Fragments in light of the Researches of New Classical Archaeology*, Leiden/Boston, 2003.

D. Altman, *Citizenship and Contemporary Direct Democracy*, Cambridge, 2019.

C.F. Arterton, *Teledemocracy*, Washington, 1987.

K.M.T. Atkinson, Athenian Legislative Procedure and Revision of Laws, *Bulletin of the John Rylands Library* 23 (1939), 107–150.

B.R. Barber, *Strong Democracy*, Berkeley, 1984.

D. Barney, *Prometheus Wired: The Hope for Democracy in the Age of Network Technology*, Vancouver, 2000.

M. Beard, Power to the People, *Times Literary Supplement* (June 29, 2016): https://www.the-tls.co.uk/articles/power-to-the-people-2/.

T. Becker, Transforming Representative Democracy: Four Real Life Experiments in Teledemocracy, in *Transformational politics. Theory, Study and Practice*, eds. S. Woolpert, C.D. Slaton and E.W. Schwerin, New York, 1998, 185–200.

T. Becker, C.D. Slaton, *The Future of Teledemocracy*, London, 2000.

J. Bentham, *A Fragment on Government (1776)*, ed. W. Harrisons, Oxford, 1960.

A. Blanshard, What Counts as the *Demos?*, *Phoenix* 58 (2004), 28–36.

J. Bodin, *The Six Bookes of a Commonweale, translated by Richard Knolles (1606)*, ed. K.D. McRae, Cambridge, 1962 (= *Les six livres de la république*, Paris, Jacques du Puis, 1576).

A. Boegehold, *The Lawcourts at Athens*, Princeton, 1995.

R. Brock, The Emergence of Democratic Ideology, *Historia* 40 (1991), 160–169.

66 *Δημοκρατία*

J. Bryce, *Modern Democracies*, London, I, 1921.

I. Budge, *The New Challenge of Direct Democracy*, Cambridge, 1996.

J. Burnheim, *Is Democracy Possible?*, Cambridge, 1985.

J. Burnheim, *The Demarchy Manifesto: For Better Public Policy*, Sydney, 2016.

D. Cammack, The Democratic Significance of the Classical Athenian Courts, in *Decline: Decadence, Decay and Decline in History and Society*, ed. W. O'Reilly, Budapest, 2017 (expected but unpublished).

D. Cammack, The *Demos* in *Demokratia*, *Classical Quarterly* 69 (2019), 42–61.

M. Canevaro, The Twilight of *Nomothesia*, *Dike* 14 (2011), 55–85.

M. Canevaro, *The Documents in the Attic Orators: Laws and Decrees in the Public Speeches of the Demosthenic 'Corpus'*, Oxford, 2013a.

M. Canevaro, *Nomothesia* in Classical Athens: What Sources Should We Believe?, *Classical Quarterly* 63 (2013b), 139–160.

M. Canevaro, Making and Changing Laws in Ancient Athens, in *Oxford Handbook of Ancient Greek Law*, eds. E.M. Harris and M. Canevaro, Oxford, 2015, 1–33: http://www.oxfordhandbooks.com/view/10.1093/oxfordhb/9780199599257.001.0001/oxfordhb-9780199599257-e-4.

M. Canevaro, The Procedure of Demosthenes' *Against Leptines*: How to Repeal (and Replace) an Existing Law?, *Journal of Hellenic Studies* 136 (2016), 39–58.

M. Canevaro, Majority Rule vs. *Consensus*: The Practice of Democratic Deliberation in the Greek *Poleis*, in *Ancient Greek History and the Contemporary Social Sciences*, eds. M. Canevaro, A. Erskine, B. Gray and J. Ober, Edinburgh, 2018, 101–156.

M. Canevaro, Laws against Laws: The Athenian Ideology of Legislation, in *Use and Abuse of Law in Athenian Courts*, eds. C. Carey and I. Giannadaki, Leiden/Boston, 2019, 271–292.

L. Carson, B. Martin, *Random Selection in Politics*, London, 1999.

P. Cartledge, *Ancient Greek Political Thought in Practice*, Cambridge, 2009.

P. Cartledge, *Democracy: A Life*, Oxford, 2016.

F. Carugati, B. Weingast, Rethinking Mass and Elite Decision-Making in the Athenian Lawcourts, in *Ancient Greek History and Contemporary Social Science*, eds. M. Canevaro, A. Erskine, B. Gray and J. Ober, Edinburgh, 2018, 157–183.

V. Cerulli Irelli, The Issue of the Legal Nature of the Constitutional Treaty and the System of Sources, in *Governing Europe under a Constitution*, eds. H.J. Blanke and S. Mangiameli, Berlin/Heidelberg, 2006, 59–64.

J. Cohen, Deliberation and Democratic Legitimacy, in *The Good Polity: Normative Analysis of the State*, eds. A. Hamlin and P. Pettit, Oxford, 1989, 17–34.

R.A. Dahl, *Democracy and Its Critics*, New Haven/London, 1989.

A. Dihle, Der Begriff des *Nomos* in der griechischen Philosophie, in *Nomos und Gesetz: Ursprünge und Wirkungen des griechischen Gesetzesdenkens*, eds. O. Behrends and W. Sellert, Göttingen, 1995, 117–134.

W. Donlan, Changes and Shifts in the Meaning of *Demos* in the Literature of the Archaic Period, *PP* 25 (1970), 381–395.

J. Dunn, *Democracy: A History*, New York, 2005.

V. Ehrenberg, *Die Rechtsidee im fruhen Griechentum: Untersuchungen zur Geschichte der werdenen Polis*, Leipzig, 1921.

C. Farrar, *The Origins of Democratic Thinking*, Cambridge, 1988.

C. Farrar, Power to the People, in *Origins of Democracy in Ancient Greece. The Invention of Politics in Classical Athens*, eds. K.A. Raaflaub, J. Ober and R.W. Wallace, Berkeley/London, 2007, 176–217.

C. Farrar, J.S. Fishkin, D. Green, C. List, R.C. Luskin, E. Levy Paluck, Disaggregating Deliberation's Effects: An Experiment within a Deliberative Poll, *British Journal of Political Science* 40 (2010), 333–347.

J. Ferejohn, Conclusion: the Citizens' Assembly Model, in *Designing Deliberative Democracy: The British Columbia Citizens' Assembly*, eds. M.E. Warren and H. Pearse, New York, 2008, 192–213.

M.I. Finley, *Democracy Ancient and Modern*, New Brunswick, 1985.

J.S. Fishkin, The Nation in a Room: Turning Public Opinion into Policy, *Boston Review* (2006): http://bostonreview.net/BR31.2/fishkin.php.

W.G. Forrest, *The Emergence of Greek Democracy*, New York, 1966.

R.B. Fuller, *No More Second-Hand God*, Garden City, 1980.

M. Gagarin, *Democratic Law in Classical Athens*, Austin, 2020.

R. Gibson, A. Römmele, S. Ward, *Electronic Democracy: Mobilisation, Organisation, and Participation via New ICTs*, London, 2004.

A.W. Gomme, *More Essays in Greek History and Literature*, Oxford, 1962.

D. Graeber, *The Democracy Project. A History, A Crisis, A Movement*, New York, 2013.

L.K. Grossman, *The Electronic Republic*, New York, 1995.

F. Gschnitzer, Zur Terminologie von Gesetz und Recht im frühen Griechisch, in *Symposion 1995*, Köln, 1997, 3–10.

M.H. Hansen, *The Sovereignty of the People's Court in Athens in the Fourth Century B.C.*, Odense, 1974.

M.H. Hansen, *Nomos* and *Psephisma* in Fourth-Century Athens, *Greek, Roman, and Byzantine Studies* 19 (1978), 315–330.

M.H. Hansen, *The Athenian Ecclesia*, Copenhagen, I, 1983.

M.H. Hansen, *Was Athens a Democracy? Popular Rule, Liberty and Equality in Ancient and Modern Political Thought*, Copenhagen, 1989a.

M.H. Hansen, *The Athenian Ecclesia*, Copenhagen, II, 1989b.

M.H. Hansen, *Solonian Democracy* in Fourth-Century Athens, *Classica et Mediaevalia* 40 (1989c), 71–99.

M.H. Hansen, The Political Powers of the Peoples Court in Fourth-Century Athens, in *The Greek City from Homer to Alexander*, eds. O. Murray and S. Price, Oxford, 1990, 239–243.

M.H. Hansen, The 2500th Anniversary of Cleisthenes' Reforms and the Tradition of Athenian Democracy, in *Ritual, Finance, Politics. Athenian Democratic Accounts Presented to David Lewis*, eds. R. Osborne and S. Homblower, Oxford, 1994, 25–37.

68   Δημοκρατία

M.H. Hansen, *Athenian Democracy in the Age of Demosthenes*, Norman, 1999.

M.H. Hansen, *The Tradition of Ancient Greek Democracy and Its Importance for Modern Democracy*, Copenhagen, 2005.

M.H. Hansen, *The Concepts of Demos, Ekklesia,* and *Dikasterion* in Classical Athens, *Greek, Roman, and Byzantine Studies* 50 (2010), 499–536.

E.M. Harris, *The Rule of Law in Action in Democratic Athens*, Oxford, 2013.

E.M. Harris, From Democracy to the Rule of Law? Constitutional Change in Athens during the Fifth and Fourth Centuries BCE, in *Die Athenische Demokratie im 4. Jahrhundert Zwischen Modernisierung und Tradition*, ed. C. Tiersch, Stuttgart, 2016, 73–88.

R. Harrison, *Democracy*, London, 1993.

C. Hignett, *A History of the Athenian Constitution to the End of the Fifth Century B.C.*, Oxford, 1952.

B. Holden, *The Nature of Democracy*, London, 1974.

B. Holden, *Understanding Liberal Democracy*, Oxford, 1988.

U. Kahrstedt, Die Nomotheten und die Legislative in Athen, *Klio* 31 (1938), 1–25.

R. Katz, *Democracy and Elections*, Oxford, 1997.

M. Kneuer, E-Democracy: A New Challenge for Measuring Democracy, *International Political Science Review* 37.5 (2016), 666–678.

H. Landemore, Inclusive Constitution-Making: The Icelandic Experiment, *The Journal of Political Philosophy* 23.2 (2015), 166–191.

A. Lanni, Judicial Review and the Athenian 'Constitution', in *Démocratie athénienne – démocratie moderne: tradition et influences*, ed. M.H. Hansen, Genève, 2010, 217–235.

J.A.O. Larsen, *Demokratia*, CPh 68 (1973), 45–46.

R. Lewanski, Institutionalising Deliberative Democracy: The Tuscany Laboratory, *Journal of Public Deliberation* 9.1 (2013), 1–14.

M.M. Markle, Jury Pay and Assembly Pay at Athens, in *Crux: Essays in Greek History*, eds. P. Cartledge and F.D. Harvey, Exeter, 1985, 265–297.

I. McLean, *Democracy and New Technology*, Cambridge, 1989.

A. Meier, L. Terán, *eDemocracy & eGovernment. Stages of a Democratic Knowledge Society*, Freibourg, 2019.

J. Miller, *Can Democracy Work? A Short History of a Radical Idea, From Ancient Athens to Our World*, New York, 2018.

D. Musti, *Demokratia. Origini di una idea*, Roma/Bari, 1995.

J. Naisbitt, *Megatrends: Ten New Directions Transforming our Lives*, New York, 1982.

J. Ober, *Mass and Elite in Democratic Athens*, Princeton, 1989.

J. Ober, *The Athenian Revolution*, Princeton, 1996.

J. Ober, I Besieged That Man: Democracy's Revolutionary Start, in *Origins of Democracy in Ancient Greece. The Invention of Politics in Classical Athens*, eds. K.A. Raaflaub, J. Ober and R.W. Wallace, Berkeley/London, 2007, 83–104.

J. Ober, The Original Meaning of 'Democracy': The Capacity to Do Things, Not Majority Rule, *Constellations* 15 (2008a), 3–9.

J. Ober, Conditions for Athenian Democracy, in *The Making and Unmaking of Democracy: Lessons from History and World Politics*, eds. T. Rabb and E. Suleiman, New York/London, 2008b, 2–22.

T. Olechowski, Von der 'Ideologie' zur 'Realität' der Demokratie, in *Hans Kelsen. Eine politikwissenschaftliche Einführung*, ed. T. Ehs, Baden-Baden/Wien, 2009, 113–132.

R. Osborne, *Athens and Athenian Democracy,* Cambridge, 2010.

M. Ostwald, *'Nomos' and the Beginnings of the Athenian Democracy*, Oxford, 1969.

M. Ostwald, *From Popular Sovereignty to the Sovereignty of Law*, Berkeley, 1986.

L. Paladin, La sovranità popolare nella democrazia degli antichi ed in quella dei moderni, in *Alle radici della democrazia. Dalla polis al dibattito costituzionale contemporaneo*, eds. A. D'Atena and E. Lanzillotta, Roma, 1998, 147–154.

P. Pasquino, Il potere diviso. Dalla *graphé paranomon* nella democrazia ateniese a John Locke e James Madison, in *Conflitti*, eds. A. Arienzo and D. Caruso, Napoli, 2005, 89–99.

P. Pasquino, Democracy Ancient and Modern: Divided Power, in *Démocratie athénienne – démocratie moderne: tradition et influences*, ed. M.H. Hansen, Genève, 2010, 1–40.

C. Pelloso, Popular Prosecution in Early Athenian Law. The Drakonian Roots of the Solonian Reforms, *Yearbook of the Research Centre for the History of Greek Law* 45 (2014–2015), 9–58.

C. Pelloso, *Ephesis eis to dikasterion: Remarks and Speculations on the Legal Nature of the Solonian Reform*, in *Symposion. Conferências sobre a História do Direito grego e helenístico (Coimbra, 1–4 Setembro 2015)*, Wien/Coimbra, 2016a, 33–48.

C. Pelloso, Coscienza nomica e scienza giuridica: un confronto tra il modello 'autoritativo' ateniese e il modello 'anarchico' romano, *Revista General De Derecho Romano* 26 (2016b), 1–47.

C. Pelloso, L'*ephesis* al tribunale popolare in diritto processuale ateniese: 'impugnazione', 'rimessione' o *tertium datur?*, *Index* 45 (2017a), 518–556.

C. Pelloso, *Nullum crimen et nulla poena sine lege*. Some Remarks on Fourth-Century Athens, *Seminarios Complutenses* 30 (2017b), 351–392.

C. Pelloso, *Nomos basileus* e potere giudicante nell'Atene del IV secolo a.C., in *'Nomos Basileus'. La regalità del diritto in Grecia antica*, eds. C. Pelloso and P. Cobetto Ghiggia, Milano/Alessandria, 2017–2018, IX–XXXVI.

D. Piovan, *Nomos basileus* o *demos basileus*? Sulla democrazia ateniese di V e IV secolo a.C., in *'Nomos Basileus'. La regalità del diritto in Grecia antica*, eds. C. Pelloso and P. Cobetto Ghiggia, Milano/Alessandria, 2017–2018, 141–154.

D. Piovan, G. Giorgini (eds.), *Brill's Companion to the Reception of Athenian Democracy From the Late Middle Ages to the Contemporary Era*, Leiden/Boston, 2021.

M. Qvortrup, *The Politics of Participation. From Athens to E-Democracy*, Manchester, 2007.

K.A. Raaflaub, The Breakthrough of *Dēmokratia* in Midfifth Century Athens, in *Origins of Democracy in Ancient Greece. The Invention of Politics in Classical Athens*, eds. K.A. Raaflaub, J. Ober and R.W. Wallace, Berkeley/London, 2007a, 105–154.

K.A. Raaflaub, Introduction, in *Origins of Democracy in Ancient Greece. The Invention of Politics in Classical Athens*, eds. K.A. Raaflaub, J. Ober and R.W. Wallace, Berkeley/London, 2007b, 1–21.

K.A. Raaflaub, Democracy, in *A Companion to the Classical Greek World*, ed. K. Kinzel, Oxford, 2008, 367–386.

P.J. Rhodes, *The Athenian Boule*, Oxford, 1972.

P.J. Rhodes, *Ancient Democracy and Modern Ideology*, London, 2003.

J.T. Roberts, *Athens on Trial*, Princeton, 1994.

G. Sartori, Democracy, in *International Encyclopaedia of the Social Science*, eds. D.L. Sills and R.K. Merton, New York, 1968, 112–121.

H.-P. Schaub, Maximising Direct Democracy by Popular Assemblies or by Ballot Votes?, *Swiss Political Science Review* 18.3 (2012), 305–331.

M. Schmidt, Institutionalising Fair Democracy: The Theory of the *Minipopulus*, *Futures* 33:3.4 (2001), 361–370.

M. Schmidt, *Direkte demokrati i Danmark. Om indførelsen af et elektronisk andetkammer*, Copenhagen, 1993.

C. Schmitt, *Constitutional Theory*, trans., Durham/London, 2008.

R. Sealey, *The Athenian Republic: Democracy or Rule of Law?*, London, 1987.

R.K. Sinclair, *Democracy and Participation in Athens*, Cambridge, 1988.

Y. Sintomer, *Le Pouvoir au Peuple: Jurys Citoyens, Tirage au Sort et Democratie Participative*, Paris, 2007.

M.J. Sundahl, The Rule of Law and the Nature of the Fourth Century Athenian Democracy, *Classica et Mediaevalia* 54 (2003), 127–129.

A. Toffler, *The Third Wave*, New York, 1980.

D. Van Reybrouck, Why Elections Are Bad for Democracy, *The Guardian* (June 29, 2016a): https://www.theguardian.com/politics/2016/jun/29/why-elections-are-bad-for-democracy.

D. Van Reybrouck, *Against Elections: The Case for Democracy*, London, 2016b.

H.J. Wolff, '*Normenkontrolle' und Gesetzesbegriff in der athenischen Demokratie. Untersuchungen zur 'graphe paranomon'*, Heidelberg, 1969.

R.P. Wolff, *In Defense of Anarchism*, New York, 1970.

S. Wolin, Norm and Form: The Constitutionalising of Democracy, in *Athenian Political Thought and the Reconstruction of American Democracy*, eds. J.P. Euben, J.R. Wallach and J. Ober, Ithaca/London, 1994, 29–58.

3 *Tribuni* and *Res Publica*

At the roots of the concurrent majority

3.1 The social contract and its Roman inspiration

As already noted in previous chapters, the belief that Western liberal and representative governments are 'pure' democracies and that democracies identify with the sovereignty of the people is undeniable.

Rather, it has become clear, at different levels of knowledge and experience, that the initial promise of democracy has been betrayed, and the rhetorical claim that government receives its authority from the people is contradicted by the fact that the government *de facto* controls and manages the people (the 'Diener' becoming 'Herren' and the 'Herren' becoming 'Diener').[1] Awareness of such semantic and historical 'deceit' and acknowledging that reality has, in fact, deviated from the archetype of democracy, in addition to a variety of other factors, including the rise of individualism, the decline of political will, the hiatus between political elites and the broader public, may better explain the crisis and the paradox of contemporary democracies. What is more, globalisation, together with privatisation and liberalisation, has radically changed the way power is seen and works. By undermining the structures established by modern constitutions to protect fundamental rights and freedom, there has been a significant weakening of the 'hierarchical paradigm' that was the backbone of the public authorities.[2]

In search of alternative models of constitutionalism, many have held Rousseau's treatise *The Social Contract* as one of the most novel and radical accounts purporting the theory of 'participatory democracy.'[3] While, on the one hand, Rousseau's brief and dense work analytically focusses on the proper place of individuals within political society, as well as on the way political institutions should be organised so as to make the citizens live and prosper in a proper 'republic,' on the other hand, the detailed description of the institutional mechanisms of the Roman republic has often been viewed not only as an inaccurate (and even useless) survey of principles[4] but also inconsistent with the idea of Rome as a purely ethical model.[5] Either *The Social Contract* represents a simply ideological work, lacking the satisfactory rigour required for this model to be approached as a coherent attempt to enact, in practice, an academic construction,[6] or it is a theorisation of democracy, which over-indulges in totalitarianism.[7] Very rarely, in other words, has Rousseau been considered a practical guide to feasible institutions.[8]

However, before we consider this further, it may prove helpful to first return to the main points of Rousseau's theoretical reconstruction, which focus on the constitutional 'positive powers' wielded by magistrates and on the 'counter-role' played by the so-called negative powers. It is noteworthy that Rousseau, on the one hand, declares in *The Social Contract* that Rome provides the key to reading his theory,[9] and on the other, he assumes in a letter to Marcet de Mézières dated 24 July 1762 that the principles established in his idea of the Republic can be reduced to just two key findings: the first that sovereignty always belongs to the people and the second that aristocracy is the best form of government. The model emerging from *The Social Contract*, in other words, depicts and grounds a different form of constitutionalism, putting forward the "ideal of the ancient *polis*" as an "alternative to the modern liberal state":[10] if Montesquieu's approach stems from the structural and functional separation of the alleged three powers of government, as well as on the technique of representation, Rousseau tends to shape sovereignty as a 'general province' that cannot be divided and delegated and does not encompass any particular, and thereby secondary, governmental function.

Some important questions arise here: How can a republic protect individuals if no separation of power takes place, as this would mean that the people is directly the sovereign but have no direct share of government? Rousseau finds an answer to this in re-reading and actualising the republican constitution of Rome and stressing the role played in such a framework by the 'tribunate': "le plus ferme appui d'une bonne constitution," with this office being both "le conservateur des lois et du pouvoir législatif," and the most effective mechanism "à protéger le souverain contre le gouvernement."[11]

It is, therefore, to Rousseau's primary source of inspiration that we must now turn our attention. Indeed, the running of the Roman republic (in line with a constitution that was always in flux)[12] was based on the suitable concurrence of co-equal and co-sovereign forces and, accordingly, on constitutional compacts as opposed to being based on established norms.[13]

3.2 The Roman tribunes

At the beginning of the Roman republic, the plebeian tribunate did not amount to a real 'constitutional power': It was a – dare I say it – curious office and a peculiar institution, especially compared to ordinary magistrates, given that it could not be counted among the integral aspects of the republican apparatus.[14]

Roman tradition links the first appointment of the tribunes, as well as the establishment of their authority, to the end of the first plebeian secession in 494 BC, less than 20 years after the foundation of the *libera res publica Romanorum*.[15] As Cicero stressed, '*Ut contra consulare imperium tribuni plebis, sic illi contra vim regiam constituti*': In other words, if a government is run by an undisputed magistracy (like early Rome was prior to the appointment of the first tribunes), it can also be called a republic but – Cicero continues – ultimately remains a monarchy. Therefore, the tribunes emerged as a counter-magistracy – that is, an office which sought to challenge the consuls' power, much in the same way that the supreme diarchic magistracy of the Roman republic was conceived of as a counter-*rex* magistracy. Shielding the plebeians from an over-dominating patrician figure, the tribunes allowed the new Roman republic to be an authentic *res publica* (entity belonging to the people) rather than a disguised monarchy.[16]

Indeed, as is common knowledge, following almost two centuries of regal rule, the Roman aristocracy rose up against the last Etruscan king and banished him.[17] The patricians who led the revolution later established a republic: a state which boasted that the *res* (i.e. the system of government) no longer belonged to a single man (the king) but to the Roman people as a whole.[18] Consequently, the chief government of the *civitas* implied the annual transfer of supreme authority from one diarchic board of patrician magistrates to another. Yet while the new supreme rulers (first labelled as *praetores* and then as *consules* or *iudices*)[19] inherited the *imperium* – as well as *omnia iura* and *omnia insignia*[20] – of the pleni-potentiary and lifetime kings,[21] they served as mere 'officers' *in potestate populi*.[22] In other words, in theory, the so-called consuls were not independent 'representatives' endowed with 'full and sufficient power.' As *magistratus populi* – that is, 'servants of the people' – they could only wield their authority in the way that a slave (*servus*) enacted the instructions of his owner (*dominus*).[23] Yet if the Romans did achieve something in 509 BC, they did not achieve much and only put another group of elites in command. The slogans repeatedly used by the new ruling order (i.e. "power to the people!," "magistrates work for the people!") were intended to mislead the lower strata of the population, or at least those citizens who, although wealthy,[24] did not participate in the government of the city. However, these slogans ultimately proved unpersuasive and, indeed, totally inadequate, to assuage the severe wrongs suffered by those Romans left out of the oligarchy in power, even though they were asked to contribute to the military defence of the city.

Immediately following the death of the banished king, Tarquin the Proud, at Cumae, the Roman *plebs* rebelled against the patricians over the thorny issues of debt, military recruitment, and distribution of land.[25] When the senators failed to meet their demands, the plebeians – who had already weaponised denial of service to resist the patricians in 498 BC[26] and for some time had been organising nocturnal meetings and secret conspiracies[27] – were prompted by Caius Sicinius Bellutus to challenge their opponents.[28] By proving to be a unified and self-conscious political body, they withdrew *en bloc* from the centre of Rome and threatened to abandon – physically and politically – the patrician-dominated *civitas* altogether. This was the first plebeian secession and stands as the archetypal example of every class struggle and revolution throughout history.[29] It was the first step towards a republican freedom understood no longer as the removal and repudiation of the monarchy but as living equality within a single *civitas* achieved through the conflict between two opposing orders and between two different ideas of *civitas*.[30]

Encamped on the Sacred Mount, or – according to conflicting accounts – on the Aventine,[31] the *plebs* entered negotiations with the *patres*: the former was able to wrest from the latter recognition of the legal co-equality and co-majesty of the two forces at stake within the new Roman republic. The result of such negotiations, sensibly directed by L. Junius Brutus and Menenius Agrippa, was, at first, a political agreement, analogous to an international treaty, by which the ruling elite granted the plebeians both debt remission and the power to appoint officials entitled to defend the members of their order. The *patres*, however, maintained the anti-monarchical institutions of their republic, recognising at the same time an alternative inner community – i.e. the plebeian one, endowed with its own magistrates acting as guarantors of the plebeian freedom.[32]

In the end, however, the plebs elected two or five officials[33] who would act as 'leaders' (*tribuni*)[34] and would help the *plebeii* in opposition to the monopolistic power held by the elite.[35] Their political resistance was aimed at curbing and preventing patrician abuses and was limited to the city: the tribunes, who, at the outset, protected citizens from violence by *intercessio* – that is, the physical interposing of their own body – were not allowed to spend the night outside the city or even to go beyond one mile from the city. Moreover, they were requested during the day to be available in the Forum and at night to leave the doors of their houses open so that the plebeians who needed assistance might have easy access to them.[36] In other words, the tribunes' office – despite being modelled after military chiefs, rather than tribal units – opposed the domination of patricians within Rome: Their first defence was not outside the city, *belli*, but inside, *domi*.[37]

If the actions and aims of the supreme plebeian leaders were of a political nature, their office – associated with the sacred[38] – differed from the patrician magistracies in the formal source of authority and in its peculiar traits.[39] While republican consuls were granted *imperium* and *auspicia*, the tribunes' power was rooted in the so-called *sacrosanctitas* of their *persona*. In fact, as of the first plebeian *lex sacrata*[40] (i.e. a unilateral resolution taken by the *plebs* in 494 BC and reinforced by a solemn and general oath in which the patricians were not formally involved)[41] until the *leges Valeriae Horatiae* were enacted in 449 BC,[42] the *tribuni plebis* functioned as a 'superstructure institution,' i.e. as an *extra ordinem* magistracy that, protected religiously by the shield of the '*sacrosanctitas*' (inviolable through the '*sacer esto* device'),[43] was beyond the common constitutional order. The body of each plebeian tribune was *sacrosanctus* by virtue of the plebeian *lex* sworn at the end of the secession and, accordingly, could not be touched, injured, or killed without incurring the wrath of the plebeian gods. So while consuls, as *magistratus populi* (servants of the whole people), were allowed to wield only the specific powers inherited from the kings, yet limited in the name of the Romans' *libertas*,[44] the tribunes, as leaders of a restricted part of the Roman people only, enjoyed a special *status* grounded in *religio*, more than on secular law. However, this did not amount to an order to protect and assist the plebeians understood either as individuals or as a class. The sacrosanctity, in other words, gave the tribunes a broader range of powers which enabled them to intervene in any action which threatened the plebeians, so as to prevent abuses and violations. The tribunes' *potestas* proved to be, in its essence, a symptomatic and permanent representation of a passive act of popular rebellion intended not to claim a direct share of sovereignty (in its proactive dimension) but to counterattack the *status quo* in such a way as to 'paralyse' the patrician government.[45]

Thus it is clear that the 5th century BC conflict in Rome's political arena was an institutionalised part of the Roman republic, not a challenge to it.[46] In this respect, the revolutionary power the tribunate was given in championing the *plebs* against the elite was essentially a form of so-called negative power, similar to that discussed in previous chapters:[47] "Car, ne pouvant rien faire, il peut tout empêcher." This was further reinforced by their great capacity to organise plebeian boycotts of military service in order to force the incumbents to make concessions or risk leaving Rome undefended against her enemies.[48] Moreover, as Cicero's portrayal of Quintus makes clear, tribunes' power was a means to refine the republic[49] but at the same time proved to be a potentially subversive device since their office was born *in seditione et ad seditionem*.[50] Likewise, Plutarch's Gracchus states that the most important duty of a tribune is to conform to the plebs' wishes and needs, more so than ethics or love of country: A tribune, protected by his sacrosanctity, might even occupy the capitol, but he was not permitted to disregard the will of his fellows, even when such will was at variance with the elite.[51]

For a long period of time, the tribunes were *de iure* not magistrates of the city[52] but rather leaders whose power the patrician elite was either *de facto* unable to contest or had the convenience of recognising, even if unwillingly.[53] The government of the city was kept in the hands of the patricians, but under the threat created by the tribunician inviolability, the plebeian leaders were able to block any actions of the patricians from taking place. Tribunes are often depicted in the sources as exercising their power of veto[54] by preventing consuls from summoning the Senate and from bringing forward laws, as well as from holding elections. They could even block the actions of the Senate and of other public officers.[55] That is to say, the tribunes functioned as a 'shield' between *patres* and plebeians, as the word *intercessio* reveals.

3.3 The Roman foundations of the Rousseauian republic

As Grell has correctly stressed, in Rousseau's political theory, Rome functions as a normative model, thereby allowing him to formulate a judgement which primarily reflects on the present.[56] Before reflecting on the Genevan thinker's peculiar view on *tribuni plebis* and *populus*, it is necessary to take into consideration Chapters 5 and 6 of Book I of *The Social Contract*. Here, Rousseau is concerned with the theoretical justification of a republic and sketches his vision for a just society, with his starting point being the premise of individualism and the idea of 'social contract' connected to the school of 'natural law.'[57] In the quest for a legitimate and reliable rule of administration in the civil order which based itself on citizens 'as they are' and laws 'as they can be,' he primarily deals with the need for an original agreement, arguing that the unequal relationship existing between masters and slaves is an inconsistent one and that a just society did not depend on the arbitrary criteria of convenience but rather on the conformation to the divine moral order.

If the social order derives from 'force,' then no proper rational *vinculum* binds the ruled and the rulers, and no legal basis exists. If the people gave themselves up to a king, there would be no instance of an authentic 'political association.' In other words, if 'the people' decide to surrender their freedom to an individual, then some form of political association must have already been created by means of an agreement that led the people out of the state of nature. In order to shape the original system (that is a system achieving the aim of reconciling social order, with individual freedom), what is needed is a form of 'partnership' which is capable of defending persons and goods with the collective force of all and under which each individual obeys no one but himself and remains as free as before.[58] What is needed is a 'contract,' the benefits and obligations of which are clear and self-evident and which becomes void in the event of a breach so that the violator immediately reverts to the system he/she was living under before: an act by which each individual is in a contract with himself/herself under the description of both natural human being and political human being. This is not a contract concluded between a people promising obedience and its magistrates promising protection, and it is not a contract which created orders for sharing authority. Individuals promised themselves, and each other, that the common good would prevail over their own personal interests.

The fundamental clause of the partnership stipulates the total alienation of one's own rights and freedoms to the community as a whole under the supreme direction of the general will.[59] Thus the conditions are the same for all, and no one can be interested in making the conditions onerous for others, as no other member of that community obtains a greater purchase on what he has given up than any other, and everyone has undergone the same sacrifice. The social contract gives life, unity, and common self, not to an 'abstract and fictitious person,' but to a collective and concrete body composed, like the Roman *populus*, by as many members as the *cives*.[60] According to Rousseau (which implicitly recalls Cicero's notion of *civitas* and *res publica*), there can only be one founding contract, which is the contract of 'partnership' (*societas*). In compliance with Roman conceptions, this partnership transforms a 'multitude' into an actual and coherent unit: 'the people.' The 'republic' – far from being a separated person from its members – is itself the hypostasis of the people and qualifies as the '*res populi*' – i.e. in terms of both denial of *regnum* (where the supreme magistrate is an arbitrary sovereign and the people are slaves) and proclamation of *libertas* (a quality consubstantial to the Roman people and to its sovereign power).[61]

In Rousseau's work, such a collective and concrete body – i.e. the people as a whole – has two main names corresponding to its different and coexisting *personae*: In an authentic 'republic,'[62] the name 'sovereign' defines it as an 'active' body and its members, who have associated as one in order to form it, are 'citizens'[63] when they are passing the laws and 'subjects' when they are subjected to them. As such, they constitute the 'state' – i.e. a term which identifies the community in its passive role only.[64] These general resolutions are binding to all, as they are made by all, with the sovereign overlapping the state (that is, each member of the political community being at once lawgiver and subject to the laws of the community).[65] Rousseau, inspired by Roman jurists, such as Ateius Capito and Gaius,[66] requires the following: No law must apply to some of the people or to some groups and not to others; no law must name individuals and use definite descriptions to single out one group for special treatment; laws are general since, like contracts, they at once bind all the parties and come from all the parties, the *cives universi*. This constitutes the only grounds for legitimacy.[67]

According to Rousseau, all in all, the sovereign's power is made up of the people. Consequently, the sovereign body cannot violate the fundamental agreement – i.e. the social contract – to which it owes its existence and by which all its constituents have the same share; moreover, sovereignty itself is nothing but the 'inalienable' and 'indivisible' exercise of the 'general will of the people,' which is deemed as always upright and always tending to the public utility (or, rather, which is the direction given by the common force of the collective body by principles that issue from it).[68] On the grounds of these requirements, it is clear that here Rousseau's main purpose is to rule out the common idea – shared also by Montesquieu and the Federalists explicitly – that sovereignty can be exercised by someone other than the people as a whole. The people constitutes the 'moral person' of the sovereign[69] and, as such, it has to make its own resolutions after determining and disclosing the general will and to act according to its decisions. Any measure taken by others out with this process cannot be attributed to the sovereign since after each individual has transferred his or her own power to the sovereign, that power cannot be delegated.[70] Rousseau claims that the idea of representation is a modern one and inseparably connected to the corruption of commercialism and finance: in a true republic (exactly like in Rome), each member of the community participates in person without being empowered to alienate or deny their right and duty to take part in the legislative proceedings. Furthermore, sovereign power cannot be divided in any way (contrary to the fundamental idea implied even in Polybios's constitutional architecture). Accordingly, there cannot be any separation of powers, with the sovereign being invested in one and only one task: to fix what the general will is and, thereby, to pass general regulations consistent with its dictates stipulated by the majority of the voting members.[71]

However, if the sovereign only has this job, it actually has no role in 'initiating' or 'implementing' the laws;[72] it does not draft proposals; it does not preside over the judgement of matters facing the community; it does not declare war; it does not execute instances of capital punishments (usually at least). It is the government – as a subordinate level of state administration – that, by means of decrees and judgements, takes practical decisions that affect the community or individuals, enacting the general will that the sovereign laws reflect. No further contract of submission to a government is necessary: Rousseau makes it clear that, by performing the contract of partnership, the people chooses a form of government and, in the quality of sovereign, it can limit, modify, and take back such governmental form as it chooses, whenever it pleases. In other words, even if a subordinate body of officials charged with all those particular matters for which the sovereign body is unsuited, the creation of a government is always open to revision.[73] An 'elected aristocracy' amounts to Rousseau's favoured system of government, as it would merge the efficiency of a small administration with the benefits of a 'delegated' democracy.[74] Outside of any contractual relationship, the sovereign would charge a small group of individuals, as endowed with a broader degree of qualities, with taking up administrative and judicial functions on its behalf: they would serve as mere 'commissaires' *in potestate populi* (and not as independent 'representatives' vested with 'full and sufficient power'), exactly in the same way that a *dominus* instructed his *servus*.[75] Yet as corroborated by Rousseau's endorsement of the 'comitial legislative procedure,'[76] this selected body of 'députés,' acting in line with the Roman *magistratus*, would pre-decide all legislation to be put before the sovereign's vote so that the magisterial initiative and the 'agenda-setting role' would give the 'aristocratic' drafters a fundamental role as 'legislative authorities' (i.e. as authorities empowered to *leges ferre*).[77]

3.4 Negative power: Its ancient paradigms and its modern versions

As explored earlier, according to Rousseau, in an 'authentic republic' (that does not correspond to an 'authentic democracy'[78]), the people is the sovereign and the sovereign passes the laws without governing and judging. Conversely, the magistrates – besides being invested in an 'agenda-setting role' within the legislative procedure – govern and judge, even if they are not the sovereign but mere enforcers of the sovereign's will (and consequently cannot pass any law).[79] This dichotomy between 'people' and 'commissaires' – that is, between 'sovereign' and 'government' – is the basic and fundamental answer that Rousseau provides to the problems concerning the abuse of power and the protection of individual liberty. As far as the sovereign is concerned, the principles of both separation and representation are excluded, whereas the government takes a subordinated place compared to the sovereign. Laws, as vehicles of the rationalised general will of the community as a whole, are the main instruments of political liberty; the absence of parliamentary assemblies rules out possible abuses carried out by the representatives against the constituents in the frame of the divide between sovereign and government. It is highly unlikely for the magistrates to have the opportunity to encroach upon the legislative power by passing general acts. Contrary to this model, and according to Montesquieu and the Founding Fathers, sovereignty is divided into three functions. The people is said to be the sovereign, but the supreme power is ultimately exercised by representatives. The executive branch is vested with a strong role in the social sphere and possesses the power to prevent laws from being passed by the legislative branch.[80]

However, against the background of such a constitutional account, one question remains: How can the sovereign prevent the government from committing abuses when the latter is formally carrying out its administrative or judicial tasks? How can the citizens' liberty be protected against governmental acts which fail to enact the general will? If, within the frame of the English model, these demands find an immediate answer in the doctrine of the separation of powers and the corrective networks of checks and balances, there is no such clear solution in the first three books of *The Social Contract*. Books I and II deal with the contractual and legislative grounds of an authentic republic, whereas Book III is concerned with the implications of this political order for the government, yet in this part of the treatise, there is no section formally dedicated to this problem. Conversely, Book IV includes three heterogenic themes which appear to be non-constructive in defining and resolving the riddle at stake – that is, a further analysis of the general will, a treatise on the virtues and the institutions of the Roman republic, and a final section regarding the civil religion. If the legacy of classical civilisation expressly represents a source of inspiration for the framework of an actualised context,[81] it is really the reading of the last book, and above all of its sections, including concrete examples drawn from Rome, that completes Rousseau's abstract theory as expounded in the previous books. In other words, the 'Roman model of public law,' which Rousseau describes at length and makes full use of, undoubtedly helps 'the judicious reader' to gain insight into a wider and deeper understanding of the rules and principles governing the authentic republic with regard not only to the articulation of powers but also to the political and constitutional instruments which seek to protect liberty.[82] The role concretely played by the tribunes through the use of their 'negative power' is brought into sharp relief in the light of both the high importance of Roman law for Rousseau's thought and the need to merge these two levels of discussion (i.e. political theory and Roman practice).

Indeed, as one scholar has recently emphasised, "during the French Revolution there were intense debates about how to divide popular sovereignty by combining a positive electoral power with an organised power of opposition," and "the idea was that the people could not remain free and in control unless they maintained a sort of 'reservoir of mistrust' in order to mount, if need be, effective opposition against a government they themselves had consecrated."[83]

As early as the 16th century, the so-called tribunician power was conceived of as a specific form of a broader power of 'resistance' and

'opposition' that, during the Reformation, emerged as the development of the Medieval theory of popular consent. Initially expressed
through the framework of religious doctrines and mainly described
in terms of non-institutionalised resistance to oppression and
tyranny – that is to say, in terms of 'direct negative power' (since it
was directly in the hands of the people) – the duty of resistance was
soon   turned   towards   political   thought   by   the   French
'Monarchomachs.'[84] These provided a stronger institutional framework for the so-called indirect negative power – that is, the 'power to
prevent abuses' not ascribed to the people, as such, but granted to
some of their officials. These officials, as champions of liberty and
guardians of the people's interests, were usually paired with the
ancient Spartan ephors,[85] a body of magistrates which Cicero himself
was inclined to qualify as the historical prototype of the Roman tribunate.[86] At the beginning of the 17th century, the idea of an institutionalised "power to prevent anti-popular conducts" found its first
complete treatise in Althusius's *Politica Methodice Digesta*. This text
definitively marks a significant step forward and qualifies as an ante-
cedent to Rousseau's conceptions of the relationship between popular sovereignty and instruments of liberty.[87] In Chapter 18, the author
deals at length with the 'democratic' body of ἔφοροι, magistrates who
do not rule but are in charge of checking the supreme magistrates
and preventing abuses of power.[88] On the grounds that the realm
does not exist for the king, but the king and any other magistrate
exist for the realm, the ἔφοροι's negative power is incorporated by
Althusius in a standard hierarchy of constitutional powers; this magisterial body, elected by the people as a 'counter-king,' is not only
granted the limited role of deposing individuals who hold public
offices in case of attempted tyranny (that is, in exceptional and radical circumstances) but also the general power to control and survey
the conduct of public authorities in order to protect the people's
interests – that is to say, over the sovereign's interest.

As of the 18th century, the question of negative power, in its two
fundamental forms, was still central to political and philosophical
debates. However, by this time, 'negative power' was no longer considered in relation to religion and was subject to an entirely political
and constitutional context: moreover, writers explicitly looked to
Roman antiquity to find paradigms of this feature, discussing –
within more or less accurate accounts of ancient institutions – how
the Roman tribunes exercised their power to veto[89] and how the
Spartan ἔφοροι were charged with overseeing, checking, and limiting

the monarchical government. Indeed, a clear-cut distinction between the (positive) 'faculty to decide' and the (negative) 'faculty to prevent' can be seen in Montesquieu's tract. In his opinion, the former represents the right to issue orders in one's own name or to correct orders issued in someone else's name, whereas the latter, deriving from the tribunician powers of the Roman republic, expresses the right to nullify a resolution taken by someone else.[90] Yet on the one hand, Montesquieu, unlike Robespierre and Rousseau, is more interested in setting limits to governmental powers than in defining the most effective devices by which the people could exercise their sovereignty, and seems to consider the (modern) doctrine of the separation of powers and the (ancient) institute of negative power as two homogenous instruments, both directed to grant constitutional equilibrium. On the other hand, criticising ancient approaches and solutions and converting the tribunician's power to veto from a counter-power against the government into a power of the government, he firmly believes that dividing the sovereign power into functions and branches is the only rational means capable of avoiding any form of predominance exercised by an absolute ruler.[91]

It is true that such a 'liberal' approach, concerned with the way power must be limited and liberty protected, certainly remains at the basis of the misfortune that, from a theoretical, practical, and historical point of view, affected Rousseau's republican model and its tribunician character. Only a few authors revived the Roman and Rousseuian ideal of an institutionalised 'negative power' by replacing the doctrine of the separation of powers with a real 'counter-power' intended to cement the liberty of the citizens.[92] The power to veto governmental acts ultimately lost its original and historical connotation, becoming, itself, a 'pro-governmental weapon' in the US constitution and in the French constitution of 1791.[93] What is more, the 'English model' codified by Montesquieu was preferred over the introduction of a modern tribunate of Rousseauian inspiration, as it is plainly attested in the constitutional debates of 1793 and in the strict position taken by Robespierre.[94] The Jacobin attitude towards absolute control proved to be inconsistent with the formal and structural bipartition of popular sovereignty (i.e. representatives' power to pass laws; tribunes' power to veto). That is to say, the idea of a parallel body legally vested with negative power, which formed an institution in place of the insurrection and was charged with preventing magisterial abuses on behalf of the people, seemed antithetical not only to the Gothic model based on representation but also to some revolutionary declensions of opposition to the *Ancien Régime*.[95] Finally, Mommsen himself, in his *Roman Public Law*, described the tribunician negative powers as an 'atypical' feature of the Roman constitution and minimised its central role, considering it instead as a testament to political dysfunction. The German jurist even ended up denying its political utility once the Roman people became an inclusive political category.[96]

3.5 The Rousseauian and Roman tribunate

It is easy to understand why Rousseau confuses 'tribunes of the people' with 'tribunes of the plebs' and why he believes that tribunician power should be restricted to negative functions which "prevent everything from being done" without "doing anything."[97] Given that his idea of sovereignty implies unity, conceiving of the tribunes as "magistrates of a section of the people" would undermine a fundamental principle of his republic. Furthermore, since in Rousseau's treatise magistrates are granted the task of submitting legislative proposals to the sovereign (that is, the people as a whole) and the sovereign passes laws as manifestations of the 'general will,' then imagining two types of magistracy (one vested with *ius agendi cum populo*, the other with *ius agendi cum plebe*) and two coexisting and opposing types of popular assemblies (the former general, the latter particular) would challenge his concept of 'law' as being intended as a general resolution that is binding to all citizens because it has been decreed by all citizens.

Accordingly, Rousseauian tribunes do not serve a class but the people as a whole (or any branch of the government if it has been threatened or oppressed). Tribunes are not vested with the power of initiating the legislative procedure; however, they do hold the power of veto. It is this tribunician function that, albeit with no share of either the legislative or the executive powers, amounts – Rousseau maintains – to the greatest of powers. In other words, in the Rousseauian republic, tribunes do not improve the system or modify the constitution by proposing bills like the correspondent plebeian magistracy was empowered to do in Rome; rather, they function only as a permanent check on the conducts of those who can threaten or harm the liberty of the citizens. Under these conditions exclusively, according to the philosopher, the tribunate would be sacred and respected as 'the protector of the laws'; only by exercising such negative power would the tribunate be an essential office as the plebeian chiefs would complete the constitution from the outside.[98]

Within this context, it is clear that Rome, together with its model of a republic, remains the main source of inspiration. Its history concretely provides a series of examples which Rousseau puts to good use in order to develop his conception of a tribunate. The Roman tribunes – who could make the proud patricians yield before a simple officer of the people who exercised neither *auspicia* nor jurisdiction – having no executive and no legislative functions, could only *de facto* 'represent' the Roman people. If, on the one hand, they were so highly revered that no one ever imagined that they could seize the sovereign power of the *populus* in its own law-making capacity,[99] on the other, on the basis of the powers entrusted to them, only by usurping the prerogatives of the Senate could they implement laws and make judgements in a governmental capacity.[100] Indeed, attuned to the excesses to which the tribunate was open by nature or by law (as attested by Roman constitutional experience), Rousseau contends that only a wisely tempered tribunate results in providing the strongest support to a good constitution. Degeneration into tyranny – he assumes – could easily occur. Even if the tribunate possesses a small amount of excess power, it could overturn everything.

Aware that no institution is beyond ill-use, Rousseau is overwhelmingly preoccupied with this possibility. Consequently, Rousseau favours devices capable of avoiding such an occurrence by compressing the tribunician sphere of action. For instance, Rousseau remarks upon how the Roman Senate kept a tight rein on the proud and restless people, and, when needed, how it even restrained the ardour of seditious tribunes, which was, in his opinion, the main cause of the collapse of the republic. Moreover, he stresses that the tribunate, like any other governmental post, is bound to weaken as its membership grows, as demonstrated by Rome, where an increasing number of tribunes used bribery, intimidation, or delusion to bar pro-plebeian actions. Rousseau explicitly blames the Roman tribunes for the fall of Rome (unlike Machiavelli and some spokesmen for the Genevan bourgeoisie).[101] In his opinion, the excessive power that they had acquired simply by decreeing that they had it, with the help of the laws created to secure liberty, served as a protective shield for the Caesars, who were the death of republican liberty.[102]

In the light of such circumstances, Rousseau goes beyond Rome and proposes a reconstruction that, at once, revives and renews the ancient tribunate. His renewed office is not a permanent instrument of 'class struggle' through which a part of the citizenry watches, limits, and/or prevents violations within the republic and against the republic. To prevent the office, in its reformed shape, from being abused and thereby from degenerating, the philosopher conceives of it as being temporary. The Rousseauian tribunate constitutes a temporary collegial body manned by a few members, which aids concertation among them, and, thus, the effectiveness of the office. Moreover, it is true that the Rousseauian reinterpretation implies that the tribunes remain as guardians of the laws and of the legislative power, yet if they fundamentally shield the sovereign against the government (as the Roman tribunes either did or were supposed to do), from *The Social Contract*, it emerges that sometimes the office supports the government against the people (as the Council of Ten did in Venice), and sometimes it is called upon to restore equilibrium or to mediate between the two integral parts of the republican constitution (as the ephors did in Sparta). The tribunate should maintain relations, serving as a middleman and connecting the government with people, and vice versa.[103]

3.6 Some conclusions

The real threat to liberty in a republic is the desire and power of the few to oppress the many. Real liberty is achievable through democratic efforts to diminish, or rather obstruct, any one body from holding excessive power, more so than by means of substantive equality. Liberty can be ensured through a conscious minority's ability to exert a counter-power against the majority within a framework of concurrent opposing powers:[104] This is the lesson which Rome has left for the future.[105]

In the 19th century, South America demonstrated the need to develop institutions which adequately defend citizens from abuses and over-domination. The procedure which emerged was a form of actualisation of Roman law through the influence played by the French democratic thinkers of the 18th century.[106]

In continuity with the modern re-reading of Roman constitutionalism, in addition to the mediation of Spanish law,[107] one of the greatest innovations in Latin America was the fast diffusion of institutes focussed on the 'Defence of the People' (*Defensoría del Pueblo*), which sought to protect human rights, as well as economic, social, and cultural liberties. Suffice it to say, Venezuela, by virtue of the constitution enacted in 1999, represents the crowning achievement of such a trend. On the one hand, the inclusion of the *Defensoría del Pueblo* within the power of the citizens gives such an office unparalleled strength; on the other hand, however, the direct connection of this office to other state powers, embedded in a system which is inherently antithetical to Montesquieu's vision and the tripartition of powers implies that the office of Defender of the People differs from the Roman tribunate (which arose as an antagonist of the patrician constitution), and, thus, fails to step towards an authentic negative power.[108]

The same limitation – i.e. a departure from the Roman tribunician model – is also evident in various European systems with the figures of the so-called protector of the citizen rights (*difensore civico*, *defensor del pueblo*, επίτροπος, *médiateur* or *défenseur des droits*, *Volksanwaltschaft*), generally linked, despite the differences that exist from system to system, to the paradigm of the Swedish 'ombudsman.'[109] Indeed, in countries where this role is deep-rooted,[110] 'civic defence' seems to play a role not so much – or at least not only – of opposition but rather of collaboration with the public administration. That is to say, this position seems to be given a positive rather than a negative power of counter-democracy, comparable to those of the tribunes. As an intermediary between citizens and public authorities, the protector of citizen rights favours out-of-court settlements for disputes. This has clear advantages for both the individuals and the administration by meeting demands for more transparency in public administration, making civil servants more responsive, and enhancing the quality of public services provided. Yet their influence and concrete successes in terms of good governance and good practices are mainly due to the ability to persuade rather than the ability to exercise clear and multifaceted apparatus of powers rooted in the law. Moreover, in most cases, civic defence, as a particular expression of a given constitutional power,[111] is only one of many other legal ways to give citizens protection and safeguard against the public administration's encroachment and misbehaviour (if not outright violations of the laws perpetrated by the judiciary), such as administrative justice or solutions to constitutional complaints: in other words, as mediator, it provides assistance more than actively countering situations.

The office of tribune disappeared at the same time as the idea of the rule of law gained prominence: an office vested with 'impeditive powers' as a genuine 'citizen right of resistance'[112] was deemed inconsistent with the liberal context of the division of powers and, consequently, was transformed into a bare constitutionality review.[113]

Privatisation of public powers and globalisation are phenomena that have revealed the inadequacy of traditional constitutionalism and made the question of the concrete protection of the fundamental

rights of the individual more relevant than ever before. In this context, the re-emergence and the updating of institutions to include
popular tribunician powers could prove an effective measure for
securing freedom under modern economic and political conditions.
Yet – one must sincerely admit – the Roman model of the tribunes of
the *plebs* (as 'class-specific officers' who cannot be appointed by the
government since their main goal is beyond the framework of the
tripartition of powers to secure rights and liberties against governmental violations and misconducts) is, without a doubt, completely
at odds with the current arrangements of representative and liberal
democracies and, therefore, would require a deep and radical rethinking of our constitutionalism, which it is not possible to sketch here.[114]

Notwithstanding this, however, it is true that on the one hand, the
factual relationship of power between the privatised public authority
and the individual is laid bare (with the overcoming of the schemes
and protections proper to administrative law and administrative justice), and on the other hand, the face-to-face confrontation of an
individual with a global actor, such as a multinational company, is
inadequate and unbalanced.

Moreover, it is undeniable that there remains a wide range of
interests concerning those who belong to the weakest strata of society that, due to their modest importance, cannot adequately be
brought into court by individuals, also taking into account the com-
plexity of rules concerning the 'class action' – i.e. a remedy that can
hardly be activated without the intercession of intermediate entities,
such as trade unions or consumer associations.

By reviving an updated version of the tribunician powers (for
instance replacing the focus of 'socio-economic class interests' with
protection of 'individual's fundamental rights'),[115] the sovereign
power, by means of the implementation of officers directly chosen
by the people, is able to find new ways to face and overcome governmental and judicial misconduct, such as abuses of power, omis-
sions or unwarranted delays of acts required by law, discriminations,
irregularities, and a wide range of acts of injustice. At the same
time, to accomplish this, we must first overcome the current 'fixation' that the ballot works as the linchpin of modern democracy,
even when it ultimately protects the social and economic elite (since
by not keeping the promises originally made, elections have failed
the people by not ensuring the liberty and security of those without
social and economic resources), and abandon the ombudsman's
general model (which, in practice, merges constitutional powers

and counter-powers through the governmental appointment of those who should be shielded from the government itself).

To keep a state from descending into oligarchy, to get through the crisis of political accountability besetting contemporary democracies, to empower and institutionalise popular contestation of elites through mechanisms that can ensure liberty for the many against the power of the few, the accepted norms of our time must be challenged. A revolution is needed (conceptual and systemic, before armed) to assault any political structure that keeps untouched (or re-enforces) the over-domination of the elite and sterilises the popular desire to avoid oppression via conflict and dissension.

As Saint Just wrote, "Que les hommes révolutionnaires soient des Romains": an imperative and inspirational motto to be born in mind as we seek to rewrite our present in order to build our most eminent future. This is just a beginning. Keep up the fight![116]

Notes

1 See Weber 1922: 172; this position is shared and enhanced by Lobrano - Onida 2016: § I.1.c. n. 18.
2 Cf. Fried 2000; Shaw 2000; Leibfried - Zürn 2005; Grimm 2010.
3 Published in 1762 as a part of a wider work on political institutions that unfortunately remained incomplete, Rousseau's *The Social Contract* (*Du Contrat Social*) undoubtedly represents one of the most influential studies in the history of political thought: a study indeed considered – in equal measure – at times provoking and inspiring, at times misleading and inconsistent: cf., *in primis*, Putterman 2010: 42 ff.; see, also, Pateman 1970: 22; 43; Barber 1984: 167 ff.; Wolfe 1985: esp. 371; Held 1996: 56. Yet cf. McCormick 2017.
4 Cousin 1964; Derathé 1964: 1494 f.
5 Leduc-Fayette 1974: 106.
6 See Burke 1949: 389; Shklar 1985: 14 f.; Constant 1988: 178; Postigliola 1992: 248 ff.; Silvestrini 2010: 19 ff.; Hatzenberger 2012.
7 Johnston 1999: 87; cf. Babbitt 1919; Chapman 1956; Talmon 1960; Crocker 1967, XVII; Labro 2010–2011.
8 Cf., paradigmatically, Putterman 2010; Lobrano 2012: 42 f.
9 Rousseau 1762: 3.127.
10 Rapaczynski 1987: 274.
11 Rousseau 1762: 4.5: "Le Tribunat n'est point une partie constitutive de la cité, et ne doit avoir aucune portion de la puissance législative ni de l'exécutif: mais c'est en cela même que la sienne est plus grande: car, ne pouvant rien faire, il peut tout empêcher. Il est plus sacré et plus révéré, comme défenseur des lois, que le prince qui les exécute, et que le souverain qui les donne. C'est ce qu'on vit bien clairement à Rome, quand ces ers patriciens, qui méprisèrent toujours le peuple entier, furent forcés de

fléchir devant un simple officier du peuple, qui n'avait ni auspices ni juri-diction." Cf. Grouchy 1555: 3.2 ff.

12 It is well-known that Roman experts of *ius publicum*, such as Cato and Cicero, were conscious of the importance of praxis in the formation pro-cess of the *status rei publicae* so as to recognise the superiority of the Roman constitution compared to those of other peoples, particularly as the organisation of Rome (*nostrae civitatis status*) had developed *rerum usu ac vetustate* over centuries and generations (Cic. *rep.* 2.9). See Cerami 1996: 10 ff.

13 Cf. Liv. 4.6.8, 27.6.2–9 (agreements between tribunes of the *plebs* and patrician magistrates); Liv. 3.31.7, 7.1.6 (agreements between tribunes of the plebs and *senatus*); Liv. 27.5.17–19, 27.6.10–11 (agreements between tribunes of the plebs and *senatus* with the subsequent intervention of the *concilia plebis*); Liv. 4.6.3, 7.21.4 (senatorial adhesions to plebeian requests); Liv. 27.6.7, 7.16.7 (agreements between *consules* and *senatus* ratified by *concilia* or *comitia*). See Cerami 2002.

14 A comprehensive analysis of the plebeian tribunate goes beyond the scope of this contribution. For some of the modern approaches concern-ing the origins of the tribunes, see Momigliano 1932; Ridley 1968; Urban 1973; Sancho Rocher 1984; Badian 1996; Smith 2012; Drogula 2017. See, moreover, Niccolini 1932 and Niccolini 1934; Bleicken 1968; Guarino 1975; Richard 1978: 435 ff.; Lobrano 1982; Thommen 1989; Lanfranchi 2015. Other general, yet helpful, accounts include Cornell 1995: 258 ff.; Lintott 1999: 121 ff.

15 Cic. *rep.* 1.48: *hanc unam rite rem publicam, id est rem populi, appellari putant. Itaque et a regum et a patrum dominatione solere in libertatem rem populi vindicari, non ex liberis populi reges requiri aut potestatem atque opes optimatium.* The traditional account concerning the rise of the Roman tribunate remains valid, regardless of personal opinion regarding the shift between *regnum* and *respublica*. On the one hand, the Roman historians and jurists believed that two annual supreme mag-istrates had always been the leaders of the state and that their govern-ment had remained essentially unchanged since 509 BC (cf. Mommsen 1887: II, 74 ff.; Bernardi 1952: 26 ff.; Capogrossi Colognesi 2009: 35; 79); on the other hand, many scholars rule out the allegedly simple tran-sition from kings to consuls as the tradition insists, believing, on the contrary, that from the expulsion of the Etruscans to as late as 367 BC, a transitional period occurred (Beloch 1926: 231 f.; De Martino 1972: 106 ff.; von Ungern-Sternberg 1990: 92 ff.; Urso 2011: 41 ff.; Drogula 2015: 40 ff.).

16 Cic. *rep.* 3.15–16: *nomen tantum videbitur regis repudiatum, res manebit, si unus omnibus reliquis magistratibus imperabit. Quare nec ephori Lacedaemone sine causa a Theopompo oppositi regibus, nec apud nos consulibus tribuni.*

17 Liv. 1.57–60, 2.1.7–11; Dion. Hal. 4.64–85.

18 Varr. *l.L.* 9.6: *populus in sua potestate, singuli in illius*; Cic. *rep.* 1.39: *est igitur, inquit Africanus, res publica res populi, populus autem non omnis hominum coetus quoquo modo congregatus, sed coetus multitudinis iuris consensu et utilitatis communione sociatus*; 1.41 *omnis civitas, quae est constitutio populi, omnis res publica, quae…populi res est*; 1.49: *quid est*

enim civitas nisi iuris societas: concilia coetusque hominum iure sociati, quae civitates appellantur; cf. Cic. *rep.* 1.47, 5.1, 6.13.

19 Zon. 7.19; Liv. 3.55.7–12.

20 Liv. 2.1.8.

21 Dion. Hal. 5.1.2 and 4.74.1; Liv. 2.1.7–8 and 8.32.3; Cic. *rep.* 2.56; D. 1.2.2.16 Pomp. *l.s. ench.*; Eutr. 1.9.1–2.

22 Cicero, preceded by Varro, described the relationship existing between *populus* and *magistratus* in the republic as the reverse to that between *rex* and *populus* in the *regnum*: cf. Cic. *de orat.* 2.167 (*magistratus in potestate populi Romani esse debent*); Cic. *pro Planc.* 62 (*sic populus Romanus deligit magistratus quasi rei publicae vilicos*); Cic. *off.* 1.124 (*est igitur proprium munus magistratus intelligere se gerere personam civitatis debereque eius dignitatem et decus sustinere, servare leges, iura discribere, ea fidei suae commissa meminisse*); cf. Cic. *pro Planc.* 11. As Lobrano 2012: 63 stresses, such a relationship would amount to a "rapporto non-contrattuale intra-potestativo gerarchico (cioè dei *cives/soci* [*domini*] *in sua potestate* con i loro *magistratus* [*servi*] *in potestate populi/domini*) noto...alla romanistica contemporanea soprattutto attraverso il rapporto del *pater-dominus* con il *filius-servus*" (cf., for further details, Lobrano 1984).

23 This implied, from the outset, limitations to wielding the *consulare imperium*: First of all, "in order to avoid the appearance of having merely substituted two kings for one, the Republic's founders arranged that the consuls should take it in turns to hold the *fasces*" (Liv. 2.1.8; Cornell 1995: 226); moreover, Valerius Publicola is said to have brought a law before the assembly giving citizens a right of *provocatio* against any capital measure pronounced by a consul (cf. Pelloso 2016, on Cic. *rep.* 2.53; Cic. *rep.* 1.62; Cic. *acad. pr.* 2.5.13; Val. Max. 4.1.1; Dion. Hal. 5.19.4 and 5.70.2; D. 1.2.2.16, 23 Pomp. *l.s. ench.*).

24 The patricians claimed to have a privileged relationship with the *auspicia* (the power of consulting the gods), a claim which justified their political and military monopolies. The idea that, at some stage, tribunes must have enjoyed the power to take public auspices for their plebiscites to become binding on the entire *populus* (Smith 2012: 263 ff.) is not persuasive. In 287 BC, the Roman people *una tantum* and unprecedently delegated to the *plebs* the ability to enact general rules: This meant that such a reform did not directly impact the procedure of voting on the plebeian resolutions; indeed, even after the *lex Hortensia* was passed, many important procedural differences continued to exist between the *iter legis* and the *iter plebissciti* (for instance, only plebeian magistrates could summon the *plebs* to make them vote, and the augural law requirements, such as the *auspicia*, did not affect the *concilia* at all: cf. Vaahtera 2001: 163; Linderski 1986: esp. 2166).

25 Cf. Sall. *hist.* 1.10 (11 M); Liv. 2.23–33; Dion. Hal. 6.22–90.

26 Dion. Hal. 5.63.2, 5.64.1–2, 5.65.1, 5.69.2: cf. Ridley 1968.

27 Liv. 2.28.1 and 2.32.1

28 Dion. Hal. 6.45, 7.33; Plut. *Cor.* 18.1–3; Liv. 3.54.12.

29 In general, as regards the historical, economical, and legal context in which the first secession and the creation of the plebeian magistracy by the *lex sacrata* occurred, cf. Serrao 2007: 13 ff.

30 On the ground of Liv. 2.44.9 (*duas civitates ex una factas, suos cuique parti magistratus, suas leges esse*) Mommsen 1887: III, 145, speaks of "die Gemeinde in der Gemeinde"; for survey of the 'state within the state' theory, see Cornell 1995: 258 ff.

31 Most sources identify the location of the first secession with the Sacred Mount, a place *trans Anienem* – that is, far from the Urbs (Cic. *Brut.* 54; Ascon. 67C; Liv. 2.32.2–33.3 and 3.54.12; Dion. Hal. 6.89; Flor. 1.17; Val. Max. 8.9.1), but some sources record it as being the Aventine Hill, a short distance from the *pomerium* but still inside the city (Liv. 2.32.3). The two alternative locations reveal the annalistic indecision in identifying the true intentions of the *plebs*: Besieging the city of patricians or founding a new city without patricians?

32 Cf. Dion. Hal. 6.87.3 and 6.89.1; Liv. 2.33.1 and 4.6.7. Ancient sources connect the end of the *secessio* to an 'agreement' or 'treaty': Liv. 2.32.1-12; Dion. Hal. 6.50–84 Flor. 1.17[23].1.2. In Livy's words: *agi deinde de concordia coeptum, concessumque in condiciones, ut plebi sui magistratus essent sacrosanti, quibus auxilii latio adversus consules essent, neve cui patrum capere eum magistratum liceret* (Liv. 2.33.1). See Catalano 1965: 30 ff.; Fiori 1996: 298, n. 25; Lanfranchi 2015: 265.

33 Livy (2.33.1–3 and 2.58.1–2) reports two different traditions as giving the original number of tribunes as two and five (cf. Dion. Hal. 6.89), whereas Diodorus (11.68.7) states that the number of tribunes was raised to four in 471 BC. On the expansion of the college to ten, see Liv. 3.30.5–7; Dion. Hal. 10.26.4–30.6; Zon. 7.17.

34 Men called military tribunes served as officers, probably of tribal units in Rome's early army. These military tribunes probably provided the model for the new plebeian tribunes: Drogula 2017: 108 f.

35 Liv. 2.31.7–9, 2.32.1–12, 2.33.1–3, 3.15.2, 3.54.12, 9.34.4, *per.* 2; Cic. *rep.* 2.58; Cic. *Brut.* 54; Cic. *Corn.* 1 fr. 49; Sall. *hist. frg.* 1.11, 3.48; Sall. *Iug.* 31.17; Sall. *ep. ad Caes.* 2.5.2; Sall. *Cat.* 33.3; Cass. Dio 4 fr. 17; Zon. 7.14; Dion. Hal. 6.45.2–3, 6.46–3, 6.83.4–5, 6.87.3, 6.89.1–2, 10.35.1; Val. Max. 8.91; App. *bell. civ.* 1.1.1–2; Plut. *Cor.* 6.1; Flor. 1.17, 1.23; D. 1.2.2.20; Oros. 2.5; Ascon 77 C. The traditional accounts – a mixture of legend and romance, most famously represented by the story of Menenius Agrippa – describe the beginning of the first plebeian secession mainly in terms of reaction to the tough measures of creditors and refusal of military service.

36 Liv. 3.20.7 and Dion. Hal. 8.8.

37 The tribunician task of protecting citizens within the city gains support from the sources stating that until 471 BC, the plebeian tribunes were originally elected by the *comitia curiata* (Pelloso 2018: 256 ff.) – i.e. an assembly consisting on 30 *curiae* (Dion. Hal. 6.89.1–2, 9.41.2; Liv. 2.56.2 and 58.1) as subdivisions of Romulus's tribes located in the city (Dion. Hal. 2.7.1–1; Plut. *Rom.* 20.2).

38 See Liv. 3.55.7–10 (even if the historian is concerned with the *lex* enacted in 449 BC): cf. Piganiol 1919.

39 See Lobrano 1972, on 'legal nature' and 'historical grounds' of the Roman tribunate; see also Serrao 1975: 26 f.; Lobrano 1982: 191 ff.

40 Liv. 3.55.10: *tribunos vetere iure iurando plebis, cum primum eam potestatem creavit, sacrosanctos esse*; Fest. s.v. '*Sacrosanctum*' (Lindsay 422);

Paul.-Fest. s.v. '*Sacrosanctum*' (Lindsay 423); Fest. s.v. '*Sacratae leges*' (Lindsay 422), Paul.-Fest. s.v. '*Sacratae leges*' (Lindsay 423), cf. Cic. *Balb.* 14.33; Cic. *leg.* 3.9; Liv. 2.33.1, 4.6.1; Dion. Hal. 6.84 and 89; Diod. 12.24. See Bleicken 1968: 3 ff.; Cornell 1995: 259; Fiori 1996: 187 ff.; 293 ff.; Liou-Gille 1997; Lintott 1999: 123 f.; Garofalo 2005: 53 ff.; Zuccotti 2007; Smith 2012: 118 ff.; Pelloso 2013: 118 ff.; Lanfranchi 2015: 257 ff.; Pellam 2015; Grillone 2017: § 5.

41 It must be highlighted that, if the patricians accepted, as a political compromise, the creation of the supreme plebeian magistracy as empowered with the so-called *auxilii latio* and as covered by the *sacrosanctitas*, the tribunes' authority was based on a public and general statute but only on the plebeian *lex sacrata*. Having elected the tribunes, the plebeians – following the proposal of Brutus – by virtue of their own *lex*, made their new leaders untouchable and swore to obey them and to shield them to the death: Dion. Hal. 6.89.1–3; cf. Liv. 2.33.1 and 3.55.8–10. After that, both plebeians and patricians swore together a further 'entrenchment clause,' providing the prohibition to modify or repeal the *lex sacrata* (cf. Dion. Hal. 6.89.4): see Fiori 1996: 314; Serrao 2007: 19; Zuccotti 2007: 526; Grillone 2017: §§ 1–6.

42 Liv. 3.55.7: *et cum religione inviolatos eos tum lege etiam fecerunt, sanciendo ut qui tribunis plebis, aedilibus, iudicibus decemviris nocuisset, eius caput Iovi sacrum esset, familia ad aedem Cereris, Liberi Liberaeque venum iret.* Indeed, the surviving accounts attest that in the first half of the 5th century, the plebeian organisation was an extralegal body which the patricians refused to recognise. The struggle for its legal acceptance was decided in 449 BC, when, in the aftermath of the second decemvirate, the Valerio-Horatian Laws re-established the plebeian organisation by virtue of a general statute: see Pelloso 2013: esp. 64 ff., and 136 ff., where Fest. s.v. '*Sacer Mons*' (Lindsay 424) is read as a confusing and imprecise reference of the *lex Valeria Horatia* – that is, the first general resolution on the plebeian tribunes (*lex tribunicia prima*) by which the Roman people, as a whole, explicitly recognised such plebeian office as a Roman magistracy.

43 The plebeian sworn resolution stipulated that anyone who harmed the tribunes automatically became *sacer* – i.e. forfeit to the plebeian gods (Liber, Libera, Ceres) – and anyone who had killed the *homo sacer* as a 'divine agent' carrying out a sacred duty incurred no penalty: Dion. Hal. 6.89.2 and Fest. s.v. '*Sacrosanctum*' (Lindsay 424). For an explanation of the so-called *sacertas* in terms of 'divine ownership,' see Albanese 1988; Garofalo 2005.

44 In general, on *libertas* see Wirszubski 1960: 133 ff.; Arena 2012: 41 ff., 50 ff.; Muroni 2013; Stolfi 2014: 139 ff. In particular, the idea of *libertas* – as the most peculiar trait of the republican system – qualifies the *populus Romanus* as belonging only to itself, whereas the *singulus* is *in potestate illius*, and the *magistratus* are 'agents' of the *civitas* of which they take on and perform the role (cf. D. 49.15.7.1; Varr. *l.L.* 9.6; Cic. *off.* 1.124; Cic. *de orat.* 2.167; Sen. *ep.* 14.7; see, moreover, Cic. *rep.* 1.39 e Tac. *ann.* 1.1.1).

45 See Lobrano 1982: 163 ff.; Catalano 2005a: 646 f. It is plausible that in the beginning, the tribunes could only protect individual plebeians from

ill-treatment and from arbitrary punishment issued by the patrician magistrates by *auxilii latio* – i.e. by giving assistance through an e*xtra ordinem* procedure in which the plebeian magistrates, either on their own initiative or on request, intervened personally (Cic. *rep.* 2.58; Cic. *leg.* 3.9; Cic. *pro Quinct.* 63; Liv. 2.33.1, 2.35.3, 3.13.6): cf. Raaflaub 1986: esp. 206. It is likely that only after the plebs obtained general recognition, the tribunes were vested with the power to 'intercede' in the procedures of the government and thus to put a stop to virtually anything. If such interventions took place in the early republic, they must have been factual expressions of a tribunician power religiously covered by the *lex sacrata* rather than the ability to exercise a legal power. Only with the settlement of 449 BC did the tribunician veto become a recognised power and, as such, a formal part of the constitution, becoming an overwhelmingly powerful device in the armoury of the plebs (Cic. *leg.* 3.7–10, 15–26; see Grosso 1977; cf. De Martino 1972: 353 f.; Richard 1978: 555 and n. 386; Lobrano 1982: 77 ff.).

46 As we know, Cicero, who writes the most important and influential treaty *de re publica* during the dark years of the great crisis suffered by Rome, claims that without a tribune, there is no republic: Cic. *rep.* 3.15–16.

47 An in-depth discussion can be found in Lobrano 1982: 85 ff. Indeed, the powers of the tribunes are largely derived from their sacrosanctity: Their status allowed them to use the office in new and different ways, expanding their role in the republic. Along this path, tribunes even found offensive uses for their inviolability, such as the abilities to arrest citizens and even incumbents and to haul them to prison: cf. Liv. 4.26.5.9; Liv. *per.* 48, 55; Cic. *Vat.* 9–10; Cic. *leg.* 3.9; Cass. Dio 37.50.

48 Ridley 1968: 543 ff.

49 Cic. *leg.* 3.15.

50 Cic. *leg.* 3.19.

51 Plut. *Ti. Gracch.* 15.2–3.

52 Cf. Plut. *Quaest. Rom.* 81. In 471 BC the patrician consul Ap. Claudius boasted that the tribunes had no authority over patricians since they were not magistrates of the people but of the plebs; they were private citizens without power (Liv. 2.56.11–12).

53 For instance, their power of arrest directly came from their inviolability. Since any physical resistance to a *tribunus* could amount to a violation of their sacrosanctity, when one of them laid hold of an individual – no matter if patricians or plebeians – the latter could not resist, as the jurist Labeo makes clear: According to the fathers of the republic, the tribunes had to be physically present to exercise the power of arrest or to order an arrest, yet they were not given the power of summons when absent (Gell. 13.12.4).

54 Cf. Liv. 2.44, 2.55, 4.6, 4.43, 4.48–50, 4.53, 4.57, 5.2, 5.9, 5.29, 6.35–39, 7.17, 8.34, 9.8, 10.9, 10.37, 25.3, 27.6, 28.45, 30.43, 31.20, 33.25, 34.1, 34.5, 34.8, 35.8, 36.40, 38.36, 38.54, 38.60, 39.4–5, 39.38, 41.6, 42.10, 43.16, 45.15, 45.21.

55 Polyb. 6.16.4–5; Liv. 6.35.10, 7.17.13, 10.9.1, 27.6.2, 43.16.6–9; Cass. Dio 37.9.4–5, 41.2.2–3. Obviously, a tribune could also veto a colleague: For instance, Tiberius Gracchus asked the plebs to remove Octavius from power after the latter was pushed by the Senate to veto the former's land

bill (cf. Badian 1972: 695 f.). See De Martino 1972: 353 f.: "L'*intercessio* poteva paralizzare la vita dello Stato. Ciò era possibile in quanto il nerbo delle forze politico-militari era plebeo e senza l'adesione od almeno la passiva acquiescenza di esse non era consigliabile per il governo patrizio intraprendere alcuna azione. Il patriziato aveva mantenuto il monopolio delle magistrature e si era assicurato il controllo del comizio, ma al di sopra della costituzione patrizia si poneva la plebe ed i *patres* non avevano una forza politica sufficiente per dominarla. Così l'*intercessio* divenne un pauroso potere costituzionale." As well-known, Sulla attempted to weaken the hated and feared tribunate through laws which sought to limit the tribunician veto (Cic. *leg.* 3.22; Cic. *Verr.* 2.1.155; Caes. *bell. civ.* 1.5, 7; Suet. *Iul.* 5). Indeed, even after the restoration of the tribunician *dignitas*, the actions of former tribunes while in office were not immune: In the year after his tribunate (75 BC), Opimius was indicted before Verres for having used his veto contrary to the *lex Cornelia*, even if, as Cicero stresses, this prosecution was a mere pretext to hit Opimius since he had publicly spoken against some noble (Cic. *Verr.* 2.1.155).

56 Grell 1995: 461.

57 Rosenblatt 2001: 2 ff.; 241 ff.

58 Rousseau 1762: 1.6: "Trouver une forme d'association, qui défende et protège de toute la force commune la personne et les biens de chaque associé, et par laquelle chacun s'unissant à tous n'obéisse pourtant qu'à lui-même et reste aussi libre qu'auparavant. Tel est le problème fondamental dont le contrat social donne la solution."

59 Riley 2001. On the relationship between freedom and subjection in Rousseau's political thought, see Wingrove 2000.

60 Gai. 1.3: *populi appellatione universi cives significantur*; cf. I.J. 1.2.4; cf. Catalano 1974: 97 ff.

61 On the divide between *regnum* and *societas*, see Cic. *rep.* 1.49: *ut ait Ennius, nulla [regni] sancta societas nec fides est*; on *regnum* as denial of liberty and on the link between *res publica* and *libertas*, see Liv. 1.17.2: *Romani veteres peregrinum regem aspernabantur. In variis voluntatibus regnari tamen omnes volebant, libertatis dulcedine nondum experta*; Liv. 2.1.1: *Libertatis autem originem inde magis quia annuum imperium consulare factum est quam quod deminutum quicquam sit ex regia potestate numeres*; cf. Varr. *l.L.* 9.6; Cic. *off.* 1.124; Cic. *rep.* 2.57; Cic. *de orat.* 2.167; Cic. *Phil.* 6.19; Sen. *ep.* 14.7; Liv. 1.56.8; Dion. Hal. 10.2; Tac. *ann.* 1.1, 3.26; D. 1.2.2.1; D. 49.15.7.1.

62 Rousseau 1762: 2.6. Irrespective of the type of government, Rousseau qualifies any state where the people is at once the source and the object of the general laws as being 'republican.' Yet it is clear that the 'whole people,' according to the philosopher, must be formally involved. The law-making process may give priority to those citizens who better understand the common good and downgrade the votes of those who are less perceptive so that the republic assures that good is realised. In Rome, as emerges from Book IV and from Rousseau's treatise of Rome's timocratically organised assembly – i.e. the *comitia centuriata* – this was achieved by weighting votes according to wealth (see McCormick 2017: 9 ff.). The 193 *centuriae* were not uniform units but varied greatly in number of

individual voters. The system was constructed in order to ensure that the decisive influence in the assembly was in the hands of the wealthy few. Even if the *proletarii* amounted to the numerical majority of the Roman citizens, they had no influence in the *comitia centuriata*, as confined to one single voting unit within the *quinta classis* of *census*. The *equites* (18 *centuriae*) and those belonging to the first timocratic *classis* (80 *centuriae*) constituted a small fraction of the entire Roman population, but they were divided into 98 *centuriae*; in other words, they were in possession of the absolute majority, making voting useless after the last *centuria* of the *prima classis* (cf. Liv. 1.42–43; Cic. *rep.* 2.39–40 [a source that was not available when Rousseau was writing]; Dion. Hal. 4.16–21 and 7.59.2–8). Rome made transparent what is now hidden by the ballot: the over-domination of the wealthiest citizens. Elections of consuls, the passing of *leges centuriatae*, and the call to war exclusively mirrored the interests and the will of the elite, even if the common people were formally involved in voting. The situation slightly changed with the reform of the 3rd century BC, when the first *centuria* called to cast its vote was to be chosen by lot among the first class (Cic. *Q. fr.* 2.14.4; Cic. *Phil.* 2.82; Liv. 24.7.12) so that the 'bandwagon effect' ceased to be of the wealthiest *centuria* (Taylor 1966: 76).

63 Rousseau 1762: 1.6: "Je n'ai pas lû que le titre de Cives ait jamais été donné aux sujets d'aucun Prince, pas même anciennement aux Macédoniens, ni de nos jours aux Anglois, quoique plus près de la liberté que tous les autres."

64 Rousseau 1762: 1.7.

65 In Rousseau's opinion, "Il n'y avait point de volonté générale sur un objet particulier," and "quand tout le people statue sur tout le peuple…c'est cet acte que j'appelle une loi" (Rousseau 1762: 2.6). See, on the eminent role played by laws in Rousseau's republic, Fralin 1978: 54; Noone 1980: 36 ff.; Waldron 1999: 31 f.

66 Gell. 10.20.2: *lex…est generale iussum populi…rogante magistratu*; cf. Gai. 1.3: *Lex est quod populus iubet atque constituit.*

67 See, on the problem concerning logical generality and equality, Noone 1980: 37 ff.; Melzer 1990: 153; *contra*, see Vaughan 1915a: 67; Putterman 2010: 11 ff.

68 Rousseau 1762: 2.3.

69 Rousseau 1762: 2.4.

70 Rousseau 1762: 3.15: "L'idée des représentants est moderne: elle nous vient du gouvernement féodal, de cet inique et absurde gouvernement dans lequel l'espèce humaine est dégradée, et où le nom d'homme est en déshonneur. Dans les anciennes républiques, et même dans les monarchies, jamais le peuple n'eut des représentants; on ne connaissait pas ce mot-là."

71 As Putterman 2010: 60 states, "Unlike the constitutional democracies in existence in contemporary Europe, there is no legislative separation or balance of powers anywhere in Rousseau's sovereignty in the sense that either of these terms (separation and balancing) mean within the parlance of modern constitutionalism. Rousseau believes in separating or balancing the powers within the executive and lauds the 'gouvernement mixte' of the English constitution, but nowhere in his writings does he

propose a constitutional separating or balancing in the traditional sense of dividing or sharing sovereignty in order to restrain it. Only acts of government can be restrained, never sovereignty." Yet if the sovereign chooses to govern, or if the magistrate wants to make laws, disorder replaces rule (cf. Rousseau 1762: 2.2 n., 3.1, 3.15). De Jouvenal 1957: 93 believes that what is most relevant is the universality or impersonality of laws, irrespective of the number of actual voters in Rousseau's state (*contra*, Putterman 2010: 27 ff.).

72 Shklar 1985: 181: "The sovereign does very little."

73 This would be nothing but a commission on behalf of the general assembly of the entire community: as Rousseau clearly states, "L'institution du gouvernement n'est point un contrat" (Rousseau 1762: 3.15): cf. Chevallier 1964: esp. 311; Bastid 1964: esp. 316; Marocco Stuardi 1990; Rosenblatt 2001: 186 f.

74 Gildin 1983: 107 f.; 110.

75 Pitkin writes that the term 'commissioner' suggests "that the representative is sent to the central government with explicit instructions, or to do a particular thing…And it is suggested that those sending him are a unified and official body…There is no doubt that…commissioners…are subordinates of those who send them" (Pitkin 1967: 134). Rather, Rousseau's account echoes what Cicero, preceded by Varro, wrote about the relationship existing between *populus* and *magistratus* (the reverse happening in the *regnum*): Cic. *de orat.* 2.167; Cic. *pro Planc.* 62; Cic. *off.* 1.124; Varr. *l.L.* 9.6. As Lobrano 2012: 63 stresses, the hierarchical and potestative relationship between citizens and magistrates would be similar to that between fathers and sons or masters and slaves (cf., for further details, Lobrano 1984).

76 Rousseau 1762: 4.4.

77 In general, on the aristocratic strands of Rousseau's thought, see Starobinski 1990: *passim*. According to Rousseau, sovereignty cannot be represented for the same reason it cannot be alienated; consequently, "les députés du peuple ne sont donc ni ne peuvent être ses représentants, ils ne sont que ses commissaires; ils ne peuvent rien conclure définitivement" (Rousseau 1762: 3.15). In another section where Rousseau deals with legislative initiation, one finds that "le simple droit de voter…rien ne peut ôter aux citoyens; et sur celui d'opiner, de proposer, de diviser, de discuter, que le gouvernement a toujours grand soin de ne laisser qu'à ses membres" (Rousseau 1762: 4.1). That "delegated power plays the greatest role in the life of the state and is kept out of citizens' sight and control" and that magistrates possess "the formal power to make decisions in the sovereign's place" (Urbinati 2006: 77; 85) is a view that cannot be shared. Rousseau's republic is not conceived of as a delegated democracy, where magistrates can overrule the sovereign and disobey the will of the people, but as an authentic republic where the sovereign and the lawgiver are the people and where magistrates work *in potestate* of the people. Notwithstanding, some authors have recently emphasised the importance of the power played by 'the few' over 'the community,' the latter being limited to acclamation for a predetermined legislative agenda fixed by the former. In other words, the authority to initiate the laws would devolve from the primeval lawgiver to a select body of elected aristocrats

whose task would be to pre-decide all legislation to be put before the people's vote (Rousseau 1762: 3.5). For instance, Johnston 1999: 87, 118 remarks that "if Rousseau's texts are read carefully," one is compelled to conclude that "the prominence of law and politics recede" since citizens turn out to be a mere "contrivance of power…an artifice to be constructed more than an essence to be realised"; see, moreover, Masters 1968: 402; Fralin 1978: 54; Gildin 1983: 159; Cohen 1986: esp. 295 f.; Melzer 1990: 237; Cullen 1993: 152 f. *Contra*, see Vaughan 1915b: 187; Cobban 1934: 91; Ellenburg 1976: 159 f.; Miller 1984: 64; Dent 1988: 172; Scott 2005.

78 As McCormick 2017: 5 ff. writes, "No, Rousseau is no democrat. He is a 'republican.'" This convincing assumption mainly derives from the following findings: "In the Social Contract, Rousseau never claims to be a democrat" and, indeed, "he is skeptical of whether democracy is practicable at all and harshly critical of actual regimes called 'democracies'"; moreover, "Rousseau emphasizes the timocratic voting structure of the republic's primary assembly, the *comitia centuriata*, an arrangement by which wealthy citizens effectively disenfranchised poorer ones" since it is "organised much differently than Athenian-style assemblies where majorities rule and one-man, one-vote prevails"; finally, "Rousseau disapproves of popular assemblies performing the tasks of both sovereignty and government, as demonstrated by his severe criticisms of the Athenian demos." Cf. 4.4: "ce qu'avait décidé le plus petit nombre passait pour une décision de la multitude, et l'on peut dire que dans les comices par centuries les affaires se réglaient à la pluralité des écus bien plus qu'à celle des voix." On the contrary, Lobrano 2012: 40 opposes "costituzionalismo '(aristocratico-)rappresentativo'" and "costituzionalismo 'democratico (-partecipativo).'"

79 On the governmental distinction between the power of giving judgement and the executive, see Melzer 1990: 205; cf. Vaughan 1915b: 63; Cobban 1934: 81 f.; Urbinati 2006: 74; Putterman 2010: 146 ff.

80 On the theoretical opposition between Rousseau and Montesquieu, see Catalano 2011: 31; cf., moreover, the recent and broad analysis by Arena 2016.

81 Cf. Rousseau 1755: XII: "Le peuple romain…ce modèle de tous les peuples libres." Cf. Wraight 2008: 20: "On the title page of *The Social Contract*, Rousseau announces himself pointedly as 'a citizen of Geneva.' He also quotes an epigram from Virgil's epic poem *The Aeneid*: '*foederis aequas dicamus leges*' – 'let us make a fair treaty.' These two elements – contemporary republican Geneva and the legacy of an enlightened classical civilization – are the wellsprings of inspiration Rousseau draws on throughout the book"; see, for a deep analysis of the topic, Rosenblatt 2001: 2 ff.

82 Cf. McCormick 2017: 9: "Commentators tend to underestimate or ignore the extent to which he wished to teach his general theory of republican government through the specific example of Rome, especially with respect to the inequitable organization of voting in the republic's primary assembly. If scholars discuss the Rome chapters at all, they usually treat Rousseau's institutional analysis as descriptive and not prescriptive; i.e., he merely reflects on the way politics was

organised in Rome, he does not recommend the republic as a model for emulation." Against the view shared by those who consider most references to Rome simply 'rhetorical devices' (Bouineau 1986), see Lobrano 2012: 44: "La scienza e la prassi giuridiche contemporanee sono caratterizzate dalla 'dimenticanza' del diritto (pubblico) romano come 'dimenticanza' di quei suoi istituti – specifici ed essenziali – che precisamente Jean-Jacques Rousseau ha, più di ogni altro, contribuito a mettere a fuoco"; Lobrano 2004: § I.1; Lobrano 2017; cf. Cousin 1964. The most eminent contributions on the topic are those written by Catalano: see Catalano 1971: 59 ff.; Catalano 1972; Catalano 1979; Catalano 1980; Catalano 1994; Catalano 1995; Catalano 2005a; Catalano 2005b; Catalano 2007: §§ 1–5.

83 Rosanvallon 2008: 122.

84 For instance, according to Calvin 1536: IV, cap. XX, § 31, the duty to resist belonged either to magistrates constituted for the defence of the people (*"sint populares magistratus ad moderandam Regum libidinem constituti quales olim erant, qui Lacedaemoniis Regibus oppositi erant Ephori: aut Romanis Consulibus Tribuni plebis: aut Atheniensium senatui Demarchi"*) or to the estates general (*"ut nunc res habent, funguntur in singulis regnis tres ordines, quum primarios conventus peragunt"*); see also Melanchthon 1530: XVI, 440; de Bèze 1574: 34. In 1557, Knox put forward a radical interpretation of the right/duty to disobey 'liberticide' authorities, severely criticising Mary Tudor under the accusation of behaving against equity and justice, of oppressing the pure, and fighting against God (Knox 1864: esp. 327). A year later, he invoked a rebellion against the idolatrous and tyrannical queen (Knox 1994). The 'negative' role played by the Spartan ephors is also highlighted by a precursor of Montesquieu (as far as the so-called Gothic forms of government). In 1574, within the framework of his renovation and development of the theory of mixed constitution, Hotman 1573: cap. X, 83 f. writes, *"Eodemque vetus illud et praeclarum Lacedaemoniorum institutum pertinuit, ut Ephoros suis Regibus attribuerent, qui (quemadmodum Plato scribit) Regibus freni instar essent, quorumque consilio atque auctoritate Reges Rempublicam administrarent."* The treatise *Vindiciae contra tyrannos* (1579), written under the pseudonym Junius Brutus and attributed to Duplessis-Mornay, is one the most important works of the Huguenot literature: It clearly shapes an institutional conception of negative power and refers it to the Spartan ephors (*'quasi imperii consortes et Regum Ephoros qui universum populi coetum repraesentant'*); Its author, describing a shared governmental power, talks of a body serving as an institutionalised check and a limit control over the royal power and emphasises the role played by the members of such body as 'public controllers,' 'guardians,' and representatives of the people (cf. Brutus 1579: 2.47, 3.91, 3.102).

85 In the Spartan mixed constitution (Plat. *Leg.* 691d–2a; *epist.* VIII 354b; Arist. *Pol.* 1265b35–40; cf. Polyb. 6.3–4, 10; Hdt. 1.65; Xen. *rep.* 11.2; Plut. *Lyc.* 7.1) the main body was the γερουσία, a senate manned by the two kings (ἀρχηγέται) as born members and 28 Spartans elected for life; laws had to be debated and voted on by the ἀπέλλα – i.e. a popular assembly; a further democratic element was represented by the members

of the board of ἔφοροι, who were yearly elected by the people from among the people themselves and were linked to the kings through a mutual monthly oath: see Richer 1998: 138 ff.; Cartledge 2000: esp. 11; Luther 2004. On the significant impact of the Spartan constitution on the political thought in the 16th and 17th centuries, see Zoli 1997: 165 f.; Rosso 2005; Nippel 2006; Vlassopoulos 2012.

86 Cic. *leg.* 3.15–16: *quare nec ephori Lacedaemone sine causa a Theopompo oppositi regibus, nec apud nos consulibus tribuni*; Cic. *rep.* 2.58: *ac ne Lycurgi quidem disciplina genuit illos in hominibus Graecis frenos; nam etiam Spartae regnante Theopompo sunt item quinque illi quos ephoros appellant, in Creta autem decem, qui cosmoe vocantur, ut contra consulare imperium tribuni plebis, sic illi contra vim regiam constituti.* Cf. Thommen 2003: esp. 19 f.; Eder 2002; Meier 2010.

87 Derathé 1950: 93; cf. von Gierke 1902: 333; Catalano 1971: 58.

88 Althusius, 1603: cap. XVIII (cf. Malandrino 2007).

89 Diderot - D'Alambert 1766: 813 (s.v. *intercessio*): "Le pouvoir & la prérogative des tribuns du peuple, & même d'un seul tribun, consistoit en ce seul mot, veto, je l'empêche, qu'ils mettoient au bas des decrets du sénat, toutes & quantes fois qu'il leur plaisoit. Ce veto étoit si puissant dans la bouche de ces magistrats plébéïens, que sans être obligés de motiver les raisons de leur opposition, intercessionis, il suffisoit pour arrêter également les résolutions du sénat, & les propositions des autres tribuns"; see also Démeunier 1788: 569.

90 Montesquieu 1748: 11.6: "J'appelle faculté de statuer, le droit d'ordonner par soi-même, ou de corriger ce qui a été ordonné par un autre. J'appelle faculté d'empêcher, le droit de rendre nulle une résolution prise par quelque autre; ce qui était la puissance des tribuns de Rome" (cf. Montesquieu 1748: 5.8). Maximilien Robespierre, on the contrary, is well aware that the two instruments at issue are conflicting alternatives, as emerges in his *Discours sur la Constitution à donner à la France* held on the 10th of May 1793: "Jusqu'ici les politiques qui ont semblé vouloir faire quelque effort, moins pour défendre la liberté que pour modifier la tyrannie, n'ont pu imaginer que deux moyens de parvenir à ce but; l'un est l'équilibre des pouvoirs, et l'autre le tribunat" (Robespierre 1866: 282). See also Rousseau that opposes the 'division du gouvernement' and the 'magistrats intermédiaires' (Rousseau 1762: 3.7); Rousseau 1782: § 7: "L'invention de cette division par Chambres ou départements est moderne. Les anciens, qui savaient mieux que nous comment se maintient la liberté, ne connurent point cet expédient. Le Sénat de Rome gouvernait la moitié du monde connu, & n'avait pas même l'idée de ces partages. Ce Sénat cependant ne parvint jamais à opprimer la puissance législative, quoique les sénateurs fussent à vie. Mais les lois avaient des Censeurs, le peuple avait des Tribuns, & le Sénat n'élisait, pas les Consuls." Cf. Catalano 1971: 59 ff. On the use of the term 'negative power' in connection with the Roman tribunes not only in the *Commentaries* written by Blackstone 1765: 154 but also in two works of Calhoun 1851 (i.e. *A Disquisition on Government* and *A Discourse on the Constitution and Government of the United States*), see Lobrano 1996: 298 and 321 ff., and Lobrano 2018: 189 f.

91 According to Montesquieu 1748: 11.6 the "distribution des trois pouvoirs" represents "le seul moyen conforme à la raison, de suppléer à la tyrannique magistrature des éphores, & aux inquisiteurs de Venise, qui sont aussi despotiques."

92 Among those who supported Rousseau's model, at first, Abbé Fauchet proposed the introduction of an elected 'moderating power,' whose task was to block any governmental act deemed as contrary to the popular general will, by issuing appeals to the sovereign for a final decision so that "the whole watches over the whole" (Fauchet 1791: esp. 60). Secondly, de Lavicomterie 1848: 84 ff. in a chapter of the treatise *Du peuple et des rois*, describes his modern version of the tribunate: guardians of the sovereignty of the people, magistrates in charge of preventing any attempt to usurp powers, tempering the institutionalised powers and granting the people's rights and liberty. Finally, Fichte – whose thought was inspired by Althusisus and Rousseau (cf. Cesa 1968: esp. 65 ff.; Catalano 1971: 91 f.) – on the one hand, conceived the ephorate in terms of "das wesentliche Bestandtheil jeder Constitution" and, on the other hand, recognised the "Volkstribunen in der römischen Republik," along "das Ephorate in der Spartanischen Verfassung," as the body that best represents his idea of "absolut negative Macht" (Fichte 1796: 208 f.): Fichte's ἔφοροι were wise men constituting an independent body appointed by the people; they had to constantly oversee the government, making inquiries even if they had no power to sit in judgement of public officials (see Rampazzo Bazzan 2017).

93 It is noteworthy that the meaning of the term 'veto' underwent a significant change: If the *Encyclopédie* used the word with reference to Roman history, Montesquieu's distinction between the power to make laws and the power to bar their implementation inspired the American and the French versions of the feature at issue. In the United States, it was used as a synonym for 'qualified negative,' and the Founding Fathers gave it the constitutional form of the power granted to the president to prevent a draft submitted to the congress (although his veto could be overridden by a two-thirds vote of both houses): historically created as a popular indirect counter-power, the veto, in the end, constituted a governmental power against the representatives of the people, according to Article I, Section 7 of the US constitution. In France, the constitution of 1791 used the word in connection with the suspensive royal sanction, empowering the king to refuse bills and withhold this assent for up to five years; then the assembly could enact the vetoed law without any further approval.

94 The idea of a constitutionalised negative power, as described in the text, clearly emerges in a proposal put forward by Hérault de Séchelles as the basis of dense debates that took place at the convention (10 June 1793): Under such a proposal, the people would exercise its sovereignty, choosing its representatives and the members of the national jury. The latter, far from being a simple shield of liberal inspiration, was thought to have a direct share of sovereignty, and any citizen could appeal to it to seek governmental action by the legislative body or executive council blocked; see Rosanvallon 2000: 66; 81. Against such a view, see the speech held on

10 May 1793 by Robespierre 1831: "C'est la tyrannie qu'il faut extirper: ce n'est pas dans les querelles de leurs maîtres que les peuples doivent chercher l'avantage de respirer quelques instants, c'est dans leur propre force qu'il faut placer la garantie de leurs droits. C'est par la même raison que je ne suis pas plus partisan de l'institution du tribunat; l'histoire ne m'a pas appris à la respecter. Je ne confie point la défense d'une si grande cause à des hommes faibles ou corruptibles; la protection des tribuns suppose l'esclavage du peuple. Je n'aime point que le peuple romain se retire sur le Mont-Sacré pour demander des protecteurs à un sénat despotique et à des patriciens insolents: je veux qu'il reste dans Rome, et qu'il en chasse tous ses tyrans. Je hais autant que les patriciens eux-mêmes et je méprise beaucoup plus ces tribuns ambitieux, ces vils mandataires du peuple, qui vendent aux grands de Rome leurs discours et leur silence, et qui ne l'ont quelquefois défendu que pour marchander sa liberté avec ses oppresseurs. Il n'y a qu'un seul tribun du peuple que je puisse avouer, c'est le peuple lui-même: c'est à chaque section de la République française que je renvoie la puissance tribunitienne; et il est facile de l'organiser d'une manière également éloignée des tempêtes de la démocratie absolue et de la perfide tranquillité du despotisme représentatif."

95 On the one hand, according to Article 35 of the *Declaration des droits de l'homme et du citoyen* of June 1793, if the government violates the rights of the people, insurrection is the most sacred and most indispensable duty. On the other hand, Robespierre rejected those approaches which supported any form of 'indirect negative power'; indeed, in his opinion, incapsulating the popular right and duty of resistance to oppression into legal schemes would be "the ultimate refinement of tyranny"; he believed in a radical and definitive form of resistance directly exercised by the people against the extreme form of power – namely, tyranny. This clearly emerges from his proposal of *Declaration des droits de l'homme et du citoyen* (24 April 1793): "Art. 29. Lorsque le gouvernement viole les droits du peuple, l'insurrection est, pour le peuple et pour chaque portion du peuple, le plus sacré des droits et le plus indispensable des devoirs; Art. 30. Quand la garantie sociale manque à un citoyen, il rentre dans le droit naturel de défendre lui-même tous ses droits; Art. 31. Dans l'un et l'autre cas, assujettir à des formes légales la résistance à l'oppression, est le dernier raffinement de la tyrannie."

96 Cf. Mommsen 1887: I, 285 ff. For a different approach, see Mommsen 1856: 251 f.; see Lobrano 1996: 341 ff.

97 Cf. Lobrano 1982: 77 ff.; 83; 130 f.; 234; Lambertini 2008: §§ 1–5; see, also, Richard 1978: 571. The powers of *auxilii latio* and *intercessio* were accompanied by the *ius agendi cum plebe* (the power to bring bills before the plebeian assemblies): The tribunes summoned and presided over the meetings of the plebs where the plebeian resolutions were passed. At first, such *plebisscita* were binding to the plebeians only, but the *lex Publilia Philonis* of 339 BC seemingly extended their application to the *populus Romanus* as a whole once the Roman Senate had ratified them through *auctoritas*. The *lex Hortensia* of 287 BC made *plebisscita*, even with no senatorial *auctoritas*, equivalent to *leges populi Romani* passed in the *comitia centuriata* or *tributa* (cf. Pelloso 2018: 272 f., n. 49 f.). Moreover, in the 2nd century BC, the tribunes were transformed into

an ordinary magistracy of the *cursus honorum* (normally held after the quaestorship) and were given the privilege to sit *in senatu*, whereas as early as the 3rd century BC, they were given the *ius senatus habendi* – i.e. the right to summon, to address, and to consult the *senatus* (cf. Lobrano 1982: 60 ff.).

 98 In his letters from the mountain, written in 1764, Rousseau criticised the use of the negative power that the Genevan Small Council (i.e. the executive branch) was claiming for itself over legislation and petitions to the General Council. Here the tribunician power transpired to be completely perverted since it was a support, not a limit, for the executive and above all since it was not directed to protect liberty and the rights of the people. See Spector 2005.

 99 Rousseau 1762: 3.12.

100 Rousseau 1762: 3.15, 4.4.

101 Cf. Rosenblatt 2001: 109 ff. The tribunician paradigm was often used within the frame of the contemporary debates concerning the Genevan constitution and, mainly, the role of the attorney general. For instance, in 1715, Chapeaurouge (*Mémoire touchant les prérogatives de la charge de Procureur Général*: AEG, MS hist 77, fols. 15v and 30) takes a position that resembles Rousseau's. Lefort (*Réponse de Monseur Louïs Le Fort* AEG, MS hist 77, fol. 34.) – seeking to protect the Genevan constitution by maintaining a balance between the councils and the people – countered that Chapeaurouge was wrong: Rome had flourished under the tribunes, and these, therefore, had to be considered the principal authors of the glory of Rome, as they assured a balance between the Senate and the people. On the contrary, cruelty and avarice brought about the republic's downfall and the Roman people's oppression (cf., for a mid-position, Chouet, *Considérations sur l'office de Procureur Général*: AEG, MS hist 77, fols. 58v and 60 that, anyway, believes that the Roman tribunes, as a dangerous example, should not be imitated). Lefort's assumption mirrors Machiavelli's claim that the appointment of the tribunes helped to stabilise the form of government in the republic since they could curb the arrogance of the nobility. Likewise, according to Montesquieu 1748: 5.11, Cicero also believed that in Rome, the republic was saved by the establishment of tribunes. From a different perspective and pursuing different goals, the Genevan attorney general Jean-Robert Tronchin (among those who condemned *The Social Contract* in 1762, as well as the author of *Lettres écrites de la campagne*) delivered a speech before the assembly of Genevan magistrates (*Discours sur l'esprit de parti*) to warn his fellows: The examples drawn from Rome proved, in his opinion, that the ambition of the leaders is the main cause of the corruption of the people and of the downfall of the state, such as when the vexations perpetrated by the patricians brought about the creation of the plebeian tribunes, who gradually stripped the senatorial class of its rights and prerogatives (Tronchin 1764: 11).

102 Rousseau 1762: 4.5. This Tacitan view (cf. Tac. *ann.* 3.27) conflicts with a long footnote included in a chapter of Book II under the title "On the Abuse of Government and Its Tendency to Degenerate" (Rousseau 1762: 3.10 n.). Here Rousseau reaffirms the natural

inclination of governments to deteriorate by becoming more restrictive or aristocratic. He then refers to the expulsion of the Tarquins as the true moment of the birth of the republic, even if, unfortunately, in that period the government had remained uncertain and up in the air, it having no firm foundations; adhering to Machiavelli's thought, Rousseau maintains that what had saved the republic was the establishment of tribunes: only after this did a real government and a true democracy take its place in Rome (cf. McCormick 2010: 237 ff., who emphasises the more populist and anti-elitist reading of the Roman republic championed by Machiavelli in his Discourses). Further on, Rousseau blames the abuses perpetrated by the aristocracy rather than the people and their tribunes for the collapse of the republic: see Millar 2002: 68 f.; Straumann 2016: 2; 30 ff.; 33; 77; 149 ff.; 278 ff.

103 At the present time, the 'democratic ideal' tends to retain an unchallenged appeal. Yet the crisis affecting the policy implied by the so-called sovereignty of parliament and, at the same time, the quest for alternative devices seeking to prevent or limit governmental encroachments and excessive discretion underpin increasingly adamant claims for a new 'participatory democracy.' In this context, democratic thinkers and activists have often found Rousseau's *The Social Contract* as an indisputable point of reference to replace the so-called English model. Through a wide-ranging discussion of republican Rome, Rousseau both develops his theory of 'republican liberty' intended as an effect of the founding social contract and depicts a 'hierarchical order' implying the priority of sovereign power over any governmental branch. Then, beyond the constitutional apparatus sketched in the aforementioned terms, he outlines an *extra ordinem* magistracy exclusively vested with negative powers and primarily serving as a 'middle term' between the executive and the legislative. If it is true that 'the people' is explicitly deemed the only sovereign and the 'technique of representation' is blamed as a feudal relic and that perverting the real concept of 'general will' conflicts with the real 'republic,' then it is equally true that Rousseau, in Book IV, dealing with the Roman main assembly, the *comitia centuriata*, highlights its timocratic method of voting (or, at least, he does not evaluate it in negative terms). As it is well-known, such methods resulted in an inegalitarian procedure which, in the normal course of events, ended up subjugating the poorer classes to the elite, embodied in the wealthier ones. Furthermore, if, unlike Montesquieu, Rousseau actualises one of the most anti-elitarian features of the Roman republic – that is, the plebeian tribunate – in *The Social Contract*, this magistracy is totally redrafted and reinvented. In Rome, the *tribuni plebis* arise as a personification of the plebeian secession, flourish as a device of elite-accountability, and serve (in their quality of public accusers, drafters of plebiscites, authorities entitled to veto) as guardians of a precise sector of the *populus*. On the contrary, in Rousseau's assessment of his republic, the tribunate is deprived of such fundamental traits so as to become something totally different from a body exclusively or primarily acting against hierarchical class domination. Rousseau (who even considers the Roman tribunate the main

cause for the downfall of the republic and for the rise of the empire) denotes his creation as a 'third' and 'heterogenous' new power. Unlike the 'sovereign' and the 'government' (as well as unlike the Roman tribunate), it does not promote actively any change in the legal system, being directed only to prevent abuses and to mediate between the constitutional powers. Unlike the 'sovereign' and the 'government' (as well as unlike the Roman tribunate), Rousseau conceives of it as a temporary institution, thus weakening its original character of permanent help. Devoted to upholding different and competing branches, sometimes the tribunate supports the people as a whole (but never a part of it only); sometimes it even supports the government, provided that the former oppresses the latter.

104　Finding the strongest support in the analysis of the tribunate of the Roman republic, in his *Disquisition on Government*, Calhoun 1851: 38 wrote, "The government of the concurrent majority, where the organism is perfect, excludes the possibility of oppression by giving to each interest, or portion, or order...the means of protecting itself by its negative against all measures calculated to advance the peculiar interest of others at its expense." It is noteworthy that the voting procedure for the United Nations Security Council amounts perhaps to the first recent example of Calhoun's "concurrent majority principle" in action. As established in Article 27 of the charter of the United Nations, a "concurring vote" of the five permanent members of the Security Council (i.e. the United States, the United Kingdom, France, the Soviet Union, and the People's Republic of China) is required, even though on substantive matters only: in fact, resolutions can only be passed with the "affirmative vote of nine members [out of 15] including the concurring votes of the permanent members." The charter gives the negative power of vetoing to each of the five permanent members, and, as it has been suggested, not only does Calhoun's political formulation accord well with the United Nations but also the unanimity principle might be partially inspired by Roman legal history, as the idea of the tribunitial negative power was so influential during the American struggles over democracy and slavery (cf. Franklin 1947; Franklin 1948).

105　See the inspiring contributions included in Trisciuoglio 2018.

106　Between 1798 and 1808, Francisco de Miranda wrote several constitutional projects inspired by the Roman *ius publicum* and the tribunate appears in his draft constitution for the provinces of the Río de la Plata (1811). In 1826, Simón Bolívar introduced the Chamber of Tribunes in Article 26 of the Bolivian constitution. In 1833 Manuel Lorenzo Vidaurre published a draft constitution which provided for the schema of powers: executive, legislative, judicial, electoral, and conservative (i.e. the tribunician power). A few years later (i.e. in 1847), the *Defensores de los pobres* were introduced in the State of San Luis Potosí (Mexico). See Catalano 1991: 35 ff.; Lobrano 1990; Maiorano 1999; Lobrano 2010; Lobrano 2011; Fernández Estrada 2014; Rubio Correa 2016. On the late-Roman *defensores civitatis* as a bridge between the *tribuni plebis* and the so-called ombudsmen currently widespread in Europe and South America, see Miglietta 2018.

107 Colomer Viadel 2013.

108 The Constitution of the Bolivarian Republic of Venezuela in 1999 framed the *Defensor* or *Defensora del Pueblo* within the traditional system of powers and the tripartition was enriched by two further aspects (Article 136): alongside the electoral power, the citizen power was divided into "Consejo Moral Republicano," "Contralor General de la República," "Fiscal General de la República," "Defensor del Pueblo" (Article 273). Cf. Spósito Contreras 2005.

109 After the decree of Charles XII who, in 1713, introduced the so-called *Högste Ombudsman*, in Sweden the *Justitieombudsman* was constitutionally recognised in 1809 as responsible for monitoring the application of laws by judges and public officials, as well as for proposing changes to the law (art. 96). This ombudsman, from being the supervisory body of the public administration, as well as of the judiciary, gradually became the advocate of individuals against any abuse perpetrated by the state or other public authorities. As a result of the creation of the *Militie Ombudsman* in 1915 and the merging of the latter with the former in 1917, there are currently four ombudsmen for justice and three further particular ombudsmen: one for children, one for equity, and one for consumers.

110 Italy is the only country in the EU Union that does not have a national 'ombudsman.' Moreover, the formal abolition of the figure of the 'municipal ombudsman' took place by virtue of article 2, paragraph 186 of Law no. 191 of 23 December 2009 (cf. the Decree-Law no. 2 of 25 January 2010, converted with amendments into Law no. 42 of 26 March 2010). Currently, ombudsmen remain at the regional level only. See Caputo 2012: 5 ff.; Guidi 2014.

111 In most countries, the 'protector of the citizens' rights' is appointed by the parliament (Sweden, Finland, Denmark, Austria, Germany, and Spain), whereas the appointment depends on the government in Greece or on the Crown in the United Kingdom, and on the president of the Republic in France. In all countries considered, the defence of the rights of the citizens is provided for in the constitution, even if in France, Austria, and Greece, it was first provided for by law and only subsequently was included in the constitution.

112 If, on the one hand, the Italian constitution (1948) rejected the idea of a right of resistance by recognising the right to strike, it granted the working class the Rousseauian power "que ne pouvant rien faire il peut tout empêcher." Indeed, by means of labour abstention, workers are directly and effectively permitted to exercise sovereignty in its negative aspect (Grosso 1952–1953; Catalano 1972; Catalano 1981: 147; 151). The right of resistance, on the contrary, was included in *Bundesrepublik Deutschland*'s *Grundgesetz* and also appears in the constitutions of Greece, Portugal, Cuba, and Paraguay.

113 Catalano 1971: 40; Catalano 1991: 42.

114 For instance, McCormick has controversially proposed to revive the tribunician function by means of the implementation of an annual commission composed of 50 members (selected by lot among the citizens and excluding individuals from the wealthiest 10%) advised by scholars and policy experts. In line with Machiavelli (more so than with

Rousseau), the new tribunes, as an add-on to the current constitution and not a replacement, would wield a threefold control on the activities carried out by the government, both institutionalising the class conflict and fostering resistance by making the people (or better one sector or class of it) aware of the oppression: Firstly, "to veto one piece of congressional legislation, one executive order, and one Supreme Court decision in the course of their one-year term"; secondly, to promote "one national referendum…over any issue they wish"; thirdly, "to initiate impeachment proceedings against one federal official from each of the three branches of government." (McCormick 2011: 183 f.). McCormick himself admits the existence of difficulties with the feasibility of his own proposal but insists that the "class-specificity" of the tribunate would "provoke and maintain a class-consciousness that would in turn, hopefully, result in further citizen participation and empowerment" (McCormick 2012: esp. 91). Cf. the scepticism showed by Hamilton 2014 about the empowerment of the people propped up by McCormick: The revival of the tribunician model achieved by updating the veto power and power of impeachment, more than the power of initiating and proposing legislation, would be "insufficient to counter the domination of elites" since the manner of empowering the people would remain "mostly reactive and thus lacking in real political power."

115 *Pace* McCormick 2011, since in Rome, many plebeians belonged to the wealthiest classes and, as such, they played an important part in the *centuriae* of the first class of *census* and could balance the influence of the patricians, the plebs cannot be identified with the poorest sectors of the population *tout court* and tribunate does not mean *per se* "protection for the poor from the oppression of the rich." The opposition is, conceptually, more between the oppressed and those who oppress than between those who govern and those who do not have a share of government.

116 Cf. Copfermann (ed.) 1968.

Bibliography

B. Albanese, *Sacer esto, Bullettino dell'Istituto di Diritto Romano* 30 (1988), 155–177.

J. Althusius, *Politica methodice digesta atque exemplis sacris et profanis illustrata,* Groningae, 1603.

V. Arena, *'Libertas' and the Practice of Politics in the Late Roman Republic,* Cambridge/New York, 2012.

V. Arena, The Roman Republic of Jean-Jacques Rousseau, *History of Political Thought* 37 (2016), 8–31.

I. Babbitt, *Rousseau and Romanticism,* New York, 1919.

E. Badian, Tiberius Gracchus and the Beginning of the Roman Revolution, in *Aufstieg und Niedergang der römischen Welt,* eds. H. Temporini and W. Haase, Berlin, I.1, 1972, 668–731.

E. Badian, *Tribuni Plebis* and *Res Publica,* in *Imperium Sine Fine: T. Robert. S. Broughton and the Roman Republic,* ed. J. Linderski, Stuttgart, 1996, 187–213.

B. Barber, *Strong Democracy: Participatory Politics for a New Age*, Berkeley, 1984.

P. Bastid, Rousseau et la théorie des formes de gouvernement, in *Études sur le Contrat social de Jean-Jacques Rousseau. Actes des journées d'étude tenues à Dijon les 3, 4, 5, et 6 mai 1962*, Paris, 1964, 315–327.

J. Beloch, *Römische Geschichte bis zum Beginn der punischen Kriege*, Berlin, 1926.

A. Bernardi, Dagli ausiliari del *rex* ai magistrati della *respublica*, *Athenaeum* 30 (1952), 3–58.

W. Blackstone, *Commentaries on the Laws of England*, London, I, 1765.

J. Bleicken, *Das Volkstribunat der klassischen Republik. Studien zu seiner Entwicklung zwischen 287 und 133 v. Chr.*, [2] Munich, 1968.

J. Bouineau, *1789–1799: Les Toges du Pouvoir ou la Révolution de Droit Antique*, Toulouse, 1986.

J. Brutus, *Vindiciae contra tyrannos, sive de Principis in populum populique in Principem legitima potesta*, Basileae (Edinburgi), 1579.

E. Burke, *Burke's Politics*, eds. R.J.S. Hoffman and P. Levack, New York, 1949.

J.C. Calhoun, *The Works*, ed. R. Crallé, Columbia, SC., I, 1851.

J. Calvin, *Institutio Christianae religionis*, Geneve, IV, 1536.

L. Capogrossi Colognesi, *Storia di Roma tra diritto e potere*, Bologna, 2009.

A. Caputo, *Un difensore civico per la repubblica. Difesa dei diritti dell'uomo e del cittadino nell'Unione Europea*, Soveria Mannelli, 2012.

P. Cartledge, Spartan Justice? Or 'The State of the Ephors'?, *Dike* 3 (2000), 5–26.

P. Catalano, *Linee del sistema sovrannazionale romano*, Torino, I, 1965.

P. Catalano, *Tribunato e resistenza*, Torino, 1971.

P. Catalano, Diritti di libertà e potere negativo. Note per l'interpretazione dell'art. 40 Cost. nella prospettiva storica, in *Studi in memoria di C. Esposito*, Padova, III, 1972, 1955–2046.

P. Catalano, *Populus Romanus Quirites,* Torino, 1974.

P. Catalano, Revolutionsauffassungen und römische Institutionen, *Klio* 61 (1979), 175–187.

P. Catalano, Un concepto olvidado: poder negativo, *Revista general de legislación y jurisprudencia* 8 (1980), 231–248.

P. Catalano, Poder negativo, in *Enciclopedia Saraiva do Direito*, Sao Paulo, LIX, 1981, 146–159.

P. Catalano, Conceptos y principios del Derecho Público Romano, de Rousseau a Bolívar, in *Constitucionalismo Latino*, Torino, I, 1991, 35–59.

P. Catalano, 'Peuple' et 'citoyens' de Rousseau à Robespierre: racines romaines du concept de république, in *Révolution et république. L'exception française*, ed. M. Vovelle, Paris, 1994, 27–36.

P. Catalano, Romanité ressuscitée et Constitution de 1793, in *L'An I et l'apprentissage de la démocratie. Actes du Colloque organisé à Saint-Ouen les 21, 22, 23, 24 juin 1993*, ed. R. Bourderon, Saint-Denis, 1995, 167–186.

P. Catalano, Sovranità della *multitudo* e potere negativo: un aggiornamento, in *Scritti in onore di G. Ferrara*, Torino, I, 2005a, 641–661.

P. Catalano, Crise de la division des pouvoirs et tribunat (le problème du pouvoir négatif), *Attualità dell'Antico* 6 (2005b), 197–227.

P. Catalano, Postilla al Promemoria, in *Diritto@Storia* 6 (2007): http://www.dirittoestoria.it/6/Memorie/Tribunato_della_Plebe/Catalano-Postilla-al-Promemoria-storico-giuridico.htm.

P. Catalano, Constitutionnalisme latin et constitution de la République romaine de 1848 (à propos du droit public romain), in *Constitutions, républiques, mémoires. 1849 entre Rome et la France*, ed. L. Reverso, Paris, 2011, 29–58.

P. Cerami, *Potere e ordinamento nell'esperienza costituzionale romana*, Torino, 1996.

P. Cerami, Prassi e convenzioni costituzionali nel sistema della *libera res publica* romana, *Annali dell'Università di Palermo* 47 (2002), 121–149.

C. Cesa, Noterelle sul pensiero politico di Fichte, *Rivista critica di storia della filosofia* 23 (1968), 62–80.

J.W. Chapman, *Rousseau, Totalitarian or Liberal?*, New York, 1956.

J.-J. Chevallier, Le mot et la notion de gouvernement chez Rousseau, in *Études sur le Contrat social de Jean-Jacques Rousseau. Actes des journées d'étude tenues à Dijon les 3, 4, 5, et 6 mai 1962*, Paris, 1964, 291–313.

A. Cobban, *Rousseau and the Modern State*, London, 1934.

J. Cohen, Reflections on Rousseau: Autonomy and Democracy, *Philosophy and Public Affairs* 15 (1986), 275–296.

A. Colomer Viadel, *El defensor del pueblo, protector de los derechos y libertades y supervisor de las administraciones públicas*, Cizur Menor, 2013.

B. Constant, *Political Writings*, trans. and ed. B. Fontana, Cambridge/London, 1988.

É. Copfermann (ed.), *Mouvement du 22 mars: Ce n'est qu'un début, continuons le combat*, Paris, 1968.

T.J. Cornell, *The Beginnings of Rome: Italy and Rome from the Bronze Age to the Punic Wars (c.1000–264 BC)*, London, 1995.

J.J. Cousin, J.-J. Rousseau interprète des institutions romaines dans le 'Contrat social', in *Études sur le Contrat social de Jean-Jacques Rousseau. Actes des journées d'étude tenues à Dijon les 3, 4, 5, et 6 mai 1962*, Paris, 1964, 13–34.

L.G. Crocker, *Jean-Jacques Rousseau: The Social Contract and Discourse on Inequality*, New York, 1967.

D.E. Cullen, *Freedom in Rousseau's Political Philosophy*, Dekalb, 1993.

T. de Bèze, *Du droit des magistrats*, Genève, 1574.

B. de Jouvenal, *Sovereignty*, Chicago/London, 1957.

L.C. de Lavicomterie, *Du peuple et des rois. Augmenté de notes et précédé d'une notice historique sur la vie et les ouvrages de l'auteur. Quatrième édition*, Paris, 1848.

F. De Martino, *Storia della costituzione romana*[2], Napoli, I, 1972.

J.N. Démeunier, *Encyclopédie méthodique, series Économie politique et diplomatique*, Paris, IV, 1788.

N.J.H. Dent, *Rousseau: An Introduction to His Psychological, Social and Political Theory*, London, 1988.

R. Derathé, *Jean-Jacques Rousseau et la science politique de son temps*, Paris, 1950.

R. Derathé (ed.), *J.J. Rousseau. Du Contrat social*, Paris, 1964.

D. Diderot, J. Le Ronde d'Alambert (eds.), *L'Encyclopédie*, Paris, VIII, 1766.

F.K. Drogula, *Commanders and Command in the Roman Republic and Early Empire*, Chapel Hill, 2015.

F.K. Drogula, Plebeian Tribunes and the Government of Early Rome, *Antichton* 51 (2017), 101–124.

W. Eder, Schlummernde Potentiale. Die Rolle von Volkstribunen und Ephoren in Verfassungskrisen, in *Widerstand, Anpassung, Integration: Die griechische Staatenwelt und Rom: Festschrift fur Jürgen Deininger zum 65. Geburtstag*, Stuttgart, 2002, 49–60.

S. Ellenburg, *Rousseau's Political Philosophy: An Interpretation from within*, Ithaca, 1976.

A. Fauchet, Treizième discours sur l'universalité d'action du Souverain dans l'État, *La Bouche de fer* 7–2 suppl. (1791), 49–60.

J.A. Fernández Estrada, *De Roma a América Latina. El tribunado del pueblo frente a la crisis de la República*, San Luis de Potosí, 2014.

J.G. Fichte, *Grundlage des Naturrechts nach Prinzipien der Wissenschaftslehre*, Jena/Leipzig, 1796.

R. Fiori, *'Homo sacer'. Dinamica politico-costituzionale di una sanzione giuridico-religiosa*, Napoli, 1996.

M. Franklin, The Roman Origin and the American Justification of the Tribunitial or Veto Power in the Charter of the United Nations, *Tulane Law Review* 22 (1947), 24–61.

M. Franklin, Problems Relating to the Influence of the Roman Idea of the Veto Power in the History of Law, *Tulane Law Review* 22 (1948), 443–458.

R. Fralin, *Rousseau and Representation: A Study of the Development of His Concept of Political Institutions*, New York, 1978.

C. Fried, Comment: Constitutionalism, Privatization, and Globalization, *Cardozo Law Review* 20 (2000), 1091–1094.

L. Garofalo, *Studi sulla sacertà*, Padova, 2005.

O. von Gierke, *Johannes Althusius und die Entwickelung der naturrechtlichen Staatstheorien*[2], Breslau, 1902.

H. Gildin, *Rousseau's Social Contract: The Design of the Argument*, Chicago, 1983.

C. Grell, *Le Dix-hutième siècle et l'antiquité en France 1680–1789*, Oxford, I, 1995.

A. Grillone, Brevi note per una conciliazione delle fonti sui fatti del 494 a.C.: alle radici del potere tribunizio, *Diritto@Storia* 15 (2017): http://www.dirittoestoria.it/15/tradizione/Grillone-Conciliazione-fonti-fatti-494-aC-Radici-potere-tribunizio.htm.

D. Grimm, The Achievement of Constitutionalism and Its Prospects in a Changed World, in *The Twilight of Constitutionalism?*, eds. P. Dobner and M. Loughlin, Oxford, 2010, 3–22.

G. Grosso, Il diritto di sciopero e l'*intercessio* dei tribuni della plebe, *Rivista italiana per le scienze giuridiche* 6–7 (1952–1953), 397–401 (= *Tradizione e misura umana del diritto*, Milano, 1976, 267–273).

G. Grosso, Appunti sulla valutazione del tribunato della plebe nella tradizione storiografica conservatrice, *Index* 7 (1977), 157–191.

N. Grouchy, *De comitiis Romanorum*, Venetiis, 1555.

A. Guarino, *La rivoluzione della plebe*, Napoli, 1975.

G. Guidi, Serve una rinnovata cultura della partecipazione ripensando alla difesa civica, *Federalismi. it* 10 (2014), 1–30.

L. Hamilton, *Freedom Is Power: Liberty through Political Representation*, Cambridge, 2014.

A. Hatzenberger, *Rousseau et l'utopie. De l'État insulaire aux cosmotopies*, Paris, 2012.

D. Held, *Theories of Democracy*, London, 1996.

F. Hotman, *Francogallia*, Genevae, 1573.

S. Johnston, *Encountering Tragedy: Rousseau and the Project of Democratic Order*, Ithaca, 1999.

J. Knox, *Apology for the Protestants* (1557), in *The Works of John Knox*, eds. D. Laing and J. Thin, Edinburgh, IV, 1864.

J. Knox, *On Rebellion*, ed. R.A. Mason, Cambridge, 1994.

C. Labro, Rousseau totalitaire contre Rousseau démocrate: enjeu et critique d'une polémique marginalisée dans l'exégèse rousseauiste des années soixante, *Etudes J.-J. Rousseau* 18 (2010–2011), 179–190.

R. Lambertini, Aspetti 'positivo' e 'negativo' della *sacrosancta potestas* dei tribuni della plebe, *Diritto@Storia* 7 (2008): http://www.dirittoestoria. it/7/Memorie/Lambertini-Positivo-negativo-potestas-Tribuni-plebe.htm.

T. Lanfranchi, *Les tribuns de la plèbe et la formation de la république romaine. 494–287 avant J.-C.*, Roma, 2015.

D. Leduc-Fayette, *Jean-Jacques Rousseau et le mythe de l'antiquité*, Paris, 1974.

S. Leibfried, M. Zürn (eds.), *Transformations of the State?*, Cambridge, 2005.

J. Linderski, The Augural Law, in *Aufstieg und Niedergang der römischen Welt*, eds. H. Temporini and W. Haase, Berlin, II.16.3, 1986, 2146–2312.

A.W. Lintott, *The Constitution of the Roman Republic*, Oxford, 1999.

B. Liou-Gille, Les *leges sacratae*: esquisse historique, *Euphrosyne* 25 (1997), 61–84.

G. Lobrano, Fondamento e natura del potere tribunizio nella storiografia giuridica contemporanea, *Index* 3 (1972), 233–262.

G. Lobrano, *Il potere dei tribuni della plebe*, Milano, 1982.

G. Lobrano, *'Pater et filius eadem persona'. Per lo studio della 'patria potestas'*, Milano, I, 1984.

G. Lobrano, *Modelo romano y constitucionalismos modernos (anotaciones en torno al debate juspublicistico contemporaneo con especial referencia a las tesis de Juan Bautista Alberti y Vittorio Emanuele Orlando)*, Bogotà, 1990.

G. Lobrano, *'Res publica res populi'. La legge e la limitazione del potere*, Torino, 1996.

G. Lobrano, La *respublica* romana, municipale-federativa e tribunizia: modello costituzionale attuale, *Diritto@Storia* 3 (2004): http://www.dirittoestoria.it/3/Memorie/Organizzare-ordinamento/Lobrano-Respublica-Romana-modello-costituzionale-attuale.htm.

G. Lobrano, A proposito dei difensori del popolo, *Diritto@Storia* 9 (2010): http://www.dirittoestoria.it/9/Memorie/Lobrano-Introduzione-a-proposito-difensor.htm.

G. Lobrano, Del defensor del pueblo al tribuno de la plebe: regreso al futuro. Un primer bosquejo de interpretación histórico-sistemática. Con atención particular al enfoque bolivariano, in *Identidad e Integración Latinoamericana y Caribeña, II Seminario en el Caribe Derecho Romano y Latinidad*, eds. P.P. Onida and E. Valdés Lobán, Napoli, 2011, 253–303.

G. Lobrano, Per la comprensione del pensiero costituzionale di J.-J. Rousseau e del diritto romano, in *Il principio della democrazia – Jean-Jacques Rousseau, Du Contrat social (1762). Nel 300° della nascita di Jean-Jacques Rousseau e nel 250° della pubblicazione del Contrat social. Atti del Seminario di Studi, Sassari, 20–21 settembre 2010*, Napoli, 2012, 39–71.

G. Lobrano, P.P. Onida, Rappresentanza o/e partecipazione. Formazione della volontà "per" o/e "per mezzo di" altri. Nei rapporti individuali e collettivi, di diritto privato e pubblico, romano e positivo, *Diritto@Storia* 14 (2016): http://www.dirittoestoria.it/14/contributi/Lobrano-Onida-Rappresentanza-o-e-partecipazione.htm.

G. Lobrano, La essenza romana del 'pensiero politico-giuridico latinoamericano'. Caratteristiche e attualità del pensiero democratico: federalismo vero contro federalismo falso tra Europa e America, in *Estudios latinoamericanos de derecho romano*, eds. J. Adame Goddard and H. Heredia Vázquez, Ciudad del México, 2017, 675–716.

G. Lobrano, "Mezzi per la difesa della libertà" e "forme di governo", in *Tribunado – Poder negativo y defensa de los derechos humanos. Segundas Jornadas Ítalo-Latinoamericanas de Defensores Cívicos y Defensores del Puebl. En homenaje al Profesor Giuseppe Grosso (Torino, 8–9 settembre 2016)*, ed. A. Trisciuoglio, Milano, 2018, 185–236.

A. Luther, *Könige und Ephoren. Untersuchungen zur spartanischen Verfassungsgeschichte*, Frankfurt a.M., 2004.

J.L. Maiorano, *El Ombudsman. Defensor del pueblo y de las instituciones republicanas*, Buenos Aires, I–IV, 1999.

C. Malandrino, L'eforato in Althusius, *Il Pensiero Politico* 40 (2007), 410–419.

D. Marocco Stuardi, Alcune osservazioni circa la distinzione tra 'souveraineté' et 'gouvernement' nella 'République' e nel 'Contrat social', *Il Pensiero Politico* 23 (1990), 19–51.

R.D. Masters, *The Political Philosophy of Rousseau*, Princeton, 1968.

J. McCormick, Greater, More Honorable and More Useful to the Republic: Plebeian Offices in Machiavelli's 'Perfect' Constitution, *I-CON* 8 (2010), 237–262.

J. McCormick, *Machiavellian Democracy*, Cambridge, 2011.

J. McCormick, Machiavellian Democracy in the Good Society, *The Good Society* 21.1 (2012), 90–117.

J. McCormick, Rousseau's Rome and the Repudiation of Populist Republicanism, *Critical Review of International Social and Political Philosophy* 10 (2017), 3–27.

M. Meier, Ephoren, Volkstribunen, Goden: Zum Aufstieg politischer 'Nebenkräfte' in Sparta, Rom und im mittelalterlichen Island, in *Zwischen Monarchie und Republik: Gesellschaftliche Stabilisierungsleistungen und politische Transformations-potentiale in den antiken Stadtstaaten*, eds. B. Linke, M. Meier and M. Strothmann, Stuttgart, 2010, 91–115.

F. Melanchthon, *Commentarii in aliquot politicos libros Aristotelis*, Witeberga, 1530.

A.M. Melzer, *The Natural Goodness of Man: On the System of Rousseau's Thought*, Chicago, 1990.

M. Miglietta, Note minime sull'origine storica e sull'"attualità" del *defensor civitatis*, in *Antologia giuridica romanistica ed antiquaria*, ed. L. Gagliardi, Milano, II, 2018.

F. Millar, *The Roman Republic in Political Thought*, Boston, 2002.

J. Miller, *Rousseau: Dreamer of Democracy*, New Haven, 1984.

A. Momigliano, Ricerche sulle magistrature romane. 3. L'origine del tribunato della plebe, in *Bullettino della Commissione Archeologica Comunale di Roma* 53 (1932), 157–177 (= in *Quarto Contributo alla storia degli studi classici e del mondo antico*, Roma, 1969, 294–313).

T. Mommsen, *Römische Geschichte*², Berlin, I, 1856.

T. Mommsen, *Römisches Staatsrecht*³, Leipzig, I–III, 1887.

Montesquieu (C.-L. de Secondat), *De l'Esprit des lois*, Geneva, 1748.

A. Muroni, Sull'origine della *libertas* in Roma antica: storiografia annalistica ed elaborazioni giurisprudenziali, *Diritto@Storia* 11 (2013): http://www.dirittoestoria.it/11/tradizione/Muroni-Origine-libertas-Roma-antica.htm.

G. Niccolini, *Il tribunato della plebe*, Milano, 1932.

G. Niccolini, *I fasti dei tribuni della plebe*, Milano, 1934.

W. Nippel, Ancient and Modern Republicanism. 'Mixed Constitution' and 'Ephors', in *The Invention of the Modern Republic*, ed. B. Fontana, Cambridge, 2006, 6–26.

J.B. Noone, *Rousseau's Social Contract*, Athens, 1980.

C. Pateman, *Participation and Democratic Theory*, Cambridge, 1970.

G. Pellam, *Sacer, sacrosanctus* and *leges sacratae, Classical Antiquity* 34 (2015), 322–334.

C. Pelloso, Sacertà e garanzie processuali in età regia e proto-repubblicana, in *Sacertà e repressione criminale in Roma arcaica*, ed. L. Garofalo, Napoli, 2013, 57–143.

C. Pelloso, *Provocatio ad populum* e poteri magistratuali dal processo all'Orazio superstite alla morte di Appio Claudio decemviro, *Studia et Documenta Historiae et Iuris* 82 (2016), 219–264.

C. Pelloso, *Ricerche sulle assemblee quiritarie*, Napoli, 2018.

A. Piganiol, Les attributions militaires et les attributions religieuses du tribunat de la plèbe, *Journal des Savants* 17 (1919), 237–248.

H.F. Pitkin, *The Concept of Representation*, Berkeley/Los Angeles/London, 1967.

A. Postigliola, *La città della ragione: Per una storia filosofica del Settecento francese*, Roma, 1992.

E. Putterman, *Rousseau, Law and the Sovereignty of the People*, Cambridge, 2010.

K.A. Raaflaub, From Protection and Defense to Offense and Participation: Stages in the Conflict of the Orders, in *Social Struggles in Archaic Rome. New Perspectives on the Conflict of the Orders*, ed. K.A. Raaflaub, Berkeley/Los Angeles/London, 1986, 198–243.

M. Rampazzo Bazzan, *Il prisma 'Rousseau': Lo sguardo di Fichte sulla politica tra Staatsrecht e Rivoluzione francese*, Milano, 2017.

A. Rapaczynski, *Nature and Politics*, Ithaca, 1987.

J.-C. Richard, *Les origines de la plèbe romaine. Essai sur la formation du dualisme patricio-plébéien*, Roma, 1978.

N. Richer, *Les éphores. Etudes sur l'histoire et sur l'image de Sparte (VIIIe-IIIe siècles av. J-Chr.)*, Paris, 1998.

R.T. Ridley, Notes on the Establishment of the Tribunate of the Plebs, *Latomus* 27 (1968), 535–558.

P. Riley, Rousseau's General Will, in *The Cambridge Companion to Rousseau*, ed. P. Riley, Cambridge, 2001, 124–153.

M. Robespierre, *Discours sur le gouvernement représentatif*, Paris, 1831.

M. Robespierre, Discours sur la Constitution à donner à la France, in *Oeuvres de Maximilien Robespierre*, ed. M. Bouloiseau et alii, Paris, 1866, 276–294.

P. Rosanvallon, *La Démocratie inachevée: Histoire de la souveraineté du peuple en France*, Paris, 2000.

P. Rosanvallon, *Counter-Democracy. Politics in an Age of Distrust*, trans., Cambridge, 2008.

H. Rosenblatt, *Rousseau and Geneva. From the First Discourse to the Social Contract, 1749–1762*, Cambridge, 2001.

M. Rosso, *La Renaissance des institutions de Sparte dans la pensée française (XVIe XVIIIe siècle)*, Aix, 2005.

J.J. Rousseau, *Discours sur l'origine et les fondements de l'inégalité parmi les hommes*, Amsterdam, 1755.

J.J. Rousseau, *Du contrat social ou principes du droit politique*, Amsterdam, 1762.

J.J. Rousseau, *Considérations sur le gouvernement de Pologne*, Londres, 1782.

M. Rubio Correa, *Ideas de la Roma antigua para modernizar las constituciones de hoy*, Lima, 2016.

L. Sancho Rocher, *El tribunado de la plebe en la Republica arcaica (491–287 A.C.)*, Zaragoza, 1984.

J.T. Scott, Rousseau's Anti-Agenda-Setting Agenda and Contemporary Democratic Theory, *American Political Science Review* 99 (2005), 137–144.

F. Serrao, *Classi, partiti e legge nella repubblica romana*, Pisa, 1975.

F. Serrao, Secessione e giuramento della plebe al monte sacro, *Index* 35 (2007), 13–26.

M. Shaw, *Theory of the Global State: Globality as an Unfinished Revolution*, Cambridge, 2000.

J.N. Shklar, *Men and Citizens: A Study of Rousseau's Social Theory*, Cambridge, 1985.

G. Silvestrini, *Diritto naturale e volontà generale. Il contrattualismo repubblicano di Jean-Jacques Rousseau*, Torino, 2010.

C.J. Smith, The Origins of the Tribunate of the Plebs, *Antichthon* 46 (2012), 101–125.

C. Spector, Droit de représentation et pouvoir négatif: la garde de la liberté dans la constitution genevoise, in *La Religion, la liberté, la justice: Un commentaire des 'Lettres écrites de la montagne' de Jean-Jacques Rousseau*, eds. B. Bernardi, F. Guénard, and G. Silvestrini, Paris, 2005, 155–172.

E. Spósito Contreras, El Derecho público romano y el constitucionalismo venezolano: comentarios a la Constitución venezolana de 1999, *Revista de Derecho del Tribunal Supremo de Justicia* 17 (2005), 391–396.

J. Starobinski, *Jean-Jacques Rousseau: Transparency and Obstruction*, trans., Chicago, 1990.

E. Stolfi, Concezioni antiche della libertà. Un primo sondaggio, *Bullettino dell'Istituto di Diritto Romano* 108 (2014), 139–178.

B. Straumann, *Crisis and Constitutionalism. Roman Political Thought from the Fall of the Republic to the Age of Revolution*, Oxford, 2016.

J.L. Talmon, *The Origins of Totalitarian Democracy*, New York, 1960.

L.R. Taylor, *Roman Voting Assemblies from the Hannibalic War to the Dictatorship of Caesar*, Ann Arbor, 1966.

L. Thommen, *Das Volkstribunat der späten römischen Republik*, Stuttgart, 1989.

L. Thommen, Volkstribunat und Ephorat. Überlegungen zum Aufseheramt in Rom und Sparta, *Göttinger Forum für Altertumswissenschaft* 6 (2003), 19–38.

A. Trisciuoglio (ed.), *Tribunado – Poder negativo y defensa de los derechos humanos. Segundas Jornadas Ítalo-Latinoamericanas de Defensores Cívicos y Defensores del Puebl. En homenaje al Profesor Giuseppe Grosso (Torino, 8–9 settembre 2016)*, Milano, 2018.

J.R. Tronchin, *Deux discours sur l'esprit de parti*, Neuchatel, 1764.

J. von Ungern-Sternberg, Die Wahrnehmung des 'Standekampfes' in der römischen Geschichtsschreibung, in *Stadt und Staatlichkeit in der frühen römischen Republik*, ed. W. Eder, Stuttgart, 1990, 92–102.

R. Urban, Zur Entstehung des Volkstribunates, *Historia* 22 (1973), 761–764.

N. Urbinati, *Representative Democracy: Principles and Genealogy*, Chicago, 2006.

G. Urso, The Origins of the Consulship in Cassius Dio's Roman History, in *Consuls and 'Res Publica'. Holding High Office in the Roman Republic*, eds. H. Beck, A. Duplá, M. Jehne and F. Pina Polo, Cambridge, 2011, 41–60.

J. Vaahtera, *Roman Augural Law in Greek Historiography: A Study of the Theory and Terminology*, Stuttgart, 2001.

C.E. Vaughan, *The Political Writings of Jean-Jacques Rousseau I*, Cambridge, 1915a.

C.E. Vaughan, *The Political Writings of Jean-Jacques Rousseau II*, Cambridge, 1915b.

K. Vlassopoulos, Sparta and Rome in Early Modern Thought: A Comparative Approach, in *Sparta in Modern Thought: Politics History and Culture*, eds. S. Hodkinson and I.M. Morris, Swansea, 2012, 43–69.

J. Waldron, *The Dignity of Legislation*, Cambridge, 1999.

M. Weber, *Wirtschaft und Gesellschaft. Grundriss der verstehenden Soziologie*, Tübingen, 1922.

E.R. Wingrove, *Rousseau's Republican Romance*, Princeton, 2000.

C. Wirszubski, *'Libertas' as a Political Idea at Rome during the Late Republic and Early Principate*, Cambridge, 1960.

J.D. Wolfe, A Defense of Participatory Democracy, *The Review of Politics* 47 (1985), 370–389.

C.D. Wraight, *Rousseau's The Social Contract. A Reader's Guide*, London, 2008.

S. Zoli, *Dall'Europa libertina all'Europa illuminista: stato laico e 'oriente' libertino nella politica e nella cultura dell'età dell'assolutismo e della Ragion di Stato da Richelieu al secolo dei lumi: alle origini del laicismo e dell'illuminismo*, Fiesole, 1997.

F. Zuccotti, Giuramento collettivo e *leges sacratae*, in *Studi per G. Nicosia*, Milano, VIII, 2007, 511–558.

Index

For Product Safety Concerns and Information please contact our EU
representative GPSR@taylorandfrancis.com
Taylor & Francis Verlag GmbH, Kaufingerstraße 24, 80331 München, Germany

www.ingramcontent.com/pod-product-compliance
Lightning Source LLC
Chambersburg PA
CBHW061752270326
41928CB00011B/2470

* 9 7 8 0 3 6 7 6 7 2 6 0 7 *